A HIGH *and* LONELY PLACE

The Sanctuary and Plight of the Cairngorms

JIM CRUMLEY

JONATHAN CAPE
LONDON

The author would like to convey special thanks to
Fred Gordon and Cameron McNeish for the best of company
in the Cairngorms.

First published 1991
© Jim Crumley 1991
Jonathan Cape, 20 Vauxhall Bridge Road, London SW1V 2SA

Jim Crumley has asserted his right
under the Copyright, Designs and Patents Act, 1988
to be identified as the author of this work

A CIP catalogue record for this book
is available from the British Library

ISBN 0–224–02682–8

Map on page 12 © Oxford Illustrators Ltd 1991

'Another Incident' from *Collected Poems* by Norman MacCaig is reproduced
by permission of The Hogarth Press; 'Fire and Ice' is taken from
The Poetry of Robert Frost, edited by Edward Connery Latham,
published by Jonathan Cape.

Printed in Great Britain by Butler & Tanner Ltd, Frome and London

To the memory of my father

Contents

Illustrations

Illustrations

Prologue

THIS BOOK IS ROOTED in a love of wild landscape. To walk in wild places – even better, just to be still in them – is to inhabit the native heath of my mind. To watch furtive lives of wild creatures unfold as they go about their own workaday business, the business of surviving, of being, is to dwell among the kinships of my spirit.

The book's landscape is the Cairngorm Mountains of Scotland, centrepiece of the eastern Highlands, a place which satisfies and delights my mind's eye with its scale, its distinctions, its shapes, its wildlife, and especially for its wildness.

My season is winter, because that is when the landscape is at its most elementally wild; because winter in the Cairngorms is a movable feast which can cover almost every month of the year; because the wildlife of the true Cairngorms winter is the mountains' most intriguing, a stoical fraternity which tholes our mightiest landscape's worst excesses or dies for the want of cunning.

But now the very mountains themselves face deaths of a kind from a winter which is not of their own making. The Cairngorms are in a state of crisis, the setting of many controversies. They are at our mercy, yours and mine.

It is the landscape's song this book sings.

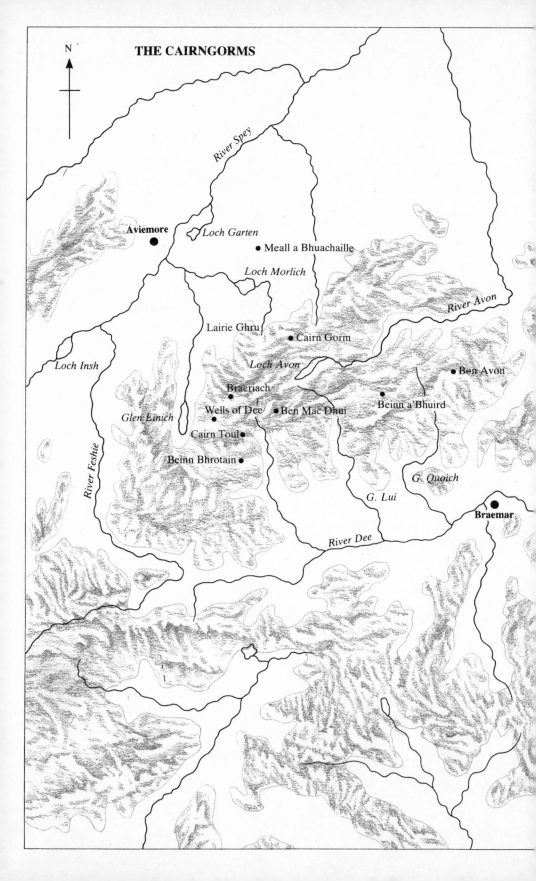

THE CAIRNGORMS

N

River Spey

Aviemore

Loch Garten

Meall a Bhuachaille

Loch Morlich

River Avon

Lairie Ghru

Cairn Gorm

Loch Insh

Loch Avon

Ben Avon

Braeriach

Beinn a'Bhuird

Wells of Dee

Ben Mac Dhui

Glen Einich

Cairn Toul

Beinn Bhrotain

G. Quoich

River Feshie

G. Lui

Braemar

River Dee

I

A Withering Landscape

A T FOUR THOUSAND FEET the flowers are half an inch high and the sparrows are white. The wind is warm whispers about the corner of a cairn. Dawn's smirry clouds have been burned dry and banished. Unfettered sun washes the crumpled boulderfield of the Cairngorms plateau, the landscape's ultimate gesture. Here, it is not the land which impresses but the skies. There are so many skies. There is so much of space.

There is no acknowledged dizzying summitry here. I have trekked instead up to an extra-terrestrial ground floor, over which the sun climbs and hovers – a flame-eyed hawk of infinite space, scrutinising prey the size of planets. Strides shorten and dawdle, shadows wither, mountains shimmer, boulders bake. So this is high summer.

For eight weeks, the Hill has panted through the longest days, cooled only in darkless night, but in a steep and slabby gouge of red rock a twenty-foot-thick wedge of tunnelled snow still limpets against the mountain. It was that kind of winter, but up here it usually is. I see in this old snow the old mountain, a small symptom of what Nan Shepherd, poet of these hills, called 'the total mountain'. Only the snow can speak to you of winter in high summer, stir in you the four-season awareness which I hold as a prerequisite to my under-standing of any landscape. I like to let my mind linger over a day such as this, then, from its zenith, pitch the same landscape headlong into winter, conjure a huge December moon to glitter down on the ice-bloated grasses at my feet.

On such a midwinter day, the mountains have reverted to type, and I find my Cairngorms addiction best served. Under snow cover, the plateau seems wider spread, further flung; it wears a harder edge too, and although there is the same absence of a clear focal point, the shallow shapes of the plateau – arcs, undulations, corrugations – are more sharply defined. But walk to the brim of Lurcher's Crag and this swan's-back world of miles-wide curves is a sudden glistening menace of angles and abysses, slab-sided and corniced, and the mind reels at the impact of its vertical depths.

The mountain shapes are huge, but blunt and undistinguished, so that they are identifiable not so much by their summits as by their sides, especially by the shapes of corries, for the Cairngorms have a repertoire of corries quite unmatched by any mountain mass in the land. In midwinter, with the snow blurring even these distinctions, with cloud storms as high as the mountains themselves welling on the horizon and dashing down in minutes and lacerating the mountain air with knife-blade winds, it is a place to taste the most primeval of mountain savours.

To walk the plateau through the brief daylight hours and watch the moon brighten and climb through the afternoon heralding the long ascendancy of night, is to be both spiritually supercharged and physically puny at the same time. Contradictions are as fundamental to the Cairngorms as corries.

By harnessing such extremes of the mountain's climate and character to a single train of thought, I widen the breadth of awareness, the range of disciplines which I try to bring to bear on the landscape. The exercise's reward is a deepening understanding, the prising free of the Cairngorms' most elusive secrets. But why bother to try and understand the landscape at all? Why not turn up, enjoy, stand and stare if you have a mind to, seek, find and go home, pleased that you came and saw and conquered, grateful perhaps that your city-beleaguered spirits were lightened, however briefly, sure in the knowledge that when you come back the hills will still be there when you need them? Is that not enough?

Look at the old snow again – snow in August! See how it dwindles, but see how it lingers. It is the characteristic, unique in our land, of the Arctic, and therein lies the desperate plight of the Cairngorms. It is an

Arctic place in the hands of people who think they live a thousand miles south of the Arctic Circle.

The governing characteristic of Arctic places is fragility, a vulnerability to change, yet change is being inflicted on the Cairngorms at a pace dictated by technologies, vested interests and commercial pressures, rather than by the mountains themselves, or even with the mountains themselves in mind. The change is not *of* the landscape, therefore it does not belong. The incomer who decries such change is often derided, but it is the change itself which is the incomer, the fish out of water. The process of change is hardly new – it has practised its indiscretions since the Victorians, and to a lesser extent even before that – but it has accelerated down the twentieth century, its increasing speed matched only by its perpetrators' recklessness and absence of responsibility. Fads of recreation and utility make fast demands on the landscape which has evolved at its own pace since the last Ice Age, which has no mechanism for recovery on such a scale. Even if every abuse of the Cairngorms were to cease tomorrow, there are places which might never recover. In the Cairngorms, nothing is commonplace, yet most of those who have addressed their problems have only commonplace solutions to offer.

No, it is not enough to come and go and be glad. It has become necessary to understand, so that those aspects of the Cairngorms which slake your wilderness thirst do not shrivel as dry as a Kalahari watering-hole when the rains do not come.

Many eyes are on the Cairngorms now. The developers, the tourist touts, the skiers, the climbers, the walkers, the naturalists, the scientists, the bureaucrats who fumble in the dark of their committee rooms for solutions, even the politicians who see votes in 'the environment' (a term blandly bandied as though it were something which affected other people) . . . all these define the landscape in their own terms.

Other eyes are on the Cairngorms too. The golden eagle presides over them, the ptarmigan cringes in his shadow, and with dotterel and golden plover and snow bunting and greenshank they eye the advancing tide of people; the white hare is thirled to the lingering snowfields of spring while alpine plants blossom tinily in the dwindling summer ooze; crested tits and ospreys and red squirrels and capercaillies wait and wonder as the ancient Caledonian pinewoods constrict; the deer and the otter and the fox, the wildcat and the dipper range high and low; the merlin hugs the ailing heather moor in his darting embrace . . . the landscape is the last refuge and strength of all of these.

There is a single fundamental truth which must be acknowledged in any assessment of the Cairngorms landscape. It is not a mountain range but a single stupendous mountain, the true summit of which is a riven, miles-wide plateau. There are no peaks, only blunt upthrusts whose cairns bear names, undulations in that bouldery granite sea. The great passes are merely troughs of the same sea. The Cairngorms impress not with their skyline but with their mass. From any neighbouring vantage point, there seems no getting round it, yet given that much of the land lies at four thousand feet, there is comparatively little spectacle. You must climb as high as the sur-rounding hills permit to learn of the grandeur of the mass. Nan Shepherd captured the phenomenon in her magical little book *The Living Mountain*:

> This can be best seen . . . from Geal Charn in the Monadhliaths which, though not even a three-thousander, stands erectly over against them across the Spey Valley. Coming steeply down its front, one watches the high panorama opposite settle into itself as one descends. It enchants like a juggler's trick. Every time I come down I want promptly to go back and see it all over again.

The trick works only because the landscape is a single crumpled mountain. It is a crucial observation because it infers that every local consequence, every small injury inflicted affects or injures the total mountain. Many of the worst exploitations in the Cairngorms have been justified on the basis of their piecemeal nature in relation to the vastness of the landmass. It is like trying to justify changing the eyes and mouth of the Mona Lisa to make her frown on the basis that only a tiny percentage of the canvas has been tampered with. The elements of the Cairngorms – river valleys, pine and birch woods, marshes and moors and lochs, foothills, passes, corries and plateaux – are the interwoven fragments of a landscape tapestry of many and rare distinctions. Deface one fragment and the uniqueness of the whole is also defaced. As threads are torn so the weave unravels. It sounds a simplistic conclusion to draw, but it is true and fundamentally relevant because, now as never before, a formidable array of forces are ranged against the Cairngorms landscape.

Skiing is only the newest and the most brash of these incursions upon nature, and arguably it is also the most devastating. A progressive spiral of the landscape's decline began in 1957 when the Forestry Commission, which had owned Cairngorm and Glen More since 1923, leased part of Cairngorm to the Cairngorm Winter Sports Development Company. Three years later the first ski road was built up into Coire Cas. Over the subsequent thirty years the territorial ambitions of the developers (now the Cairngorm Chairlift Company) have advanced right across the Northern Corries from Coire na Ciste in the east to Lurcher's Gully in the west. Chairlifts, ski-tows, restaurants, car parks were built in Coire Cas in the early 1960s, followed by the grotesquely purpose-built Aviemore Centre, the fatal wedding of skiing development to tourism from which the mountains have suffered ever since. More development followed on the mountain – the Ptarmigan Restaurant near the summit of Cairngorm and a new road, new car parks, restaurant and chairlifts were all in operation in Coire na Ciste by the mid-1970s.

Two things happened in the midst of all this to underline attitudes within the Scottish Office to what was happening to a landscape judged by scientists around the world to be the one most worthy of thoughtful conservation in the whole of Britain. The first was that in 1967 (the year before the Ptarmigan Restaurant was built) a Scottish Development Department report expressed concern for the future of the Cairngorm plateau, which already had begun to deteriorate under pressure of development. Five years later, during which time no shred of remedial conservation action was taken, the Scottish Office compelled the Forestry Commission to hand Cairngorm over to the Highlands and Islands Development Board, with the result that the most vulnerable part of the landscape was now in the hands of a Government organisation whose brief was not to conserve but to develop.

The second half of the seventies saw a number of bureaucratic endeavours put forward, notably by Grampian Regional Council and the Countryside Commission for Scotland, to introduce a measure of control, but none bore fruit. The 1980s simply spread the conflict westward. A public inquiry rejected proposals to develop in Lurcher's Gully, wildest of all the northern corries of Cairngorm, but that conflict rumbled right through the decade, marking a nadir in relations between the Chairlift Company and conservationists. One revised proposal included a road right across from Coire Cas to Lurcher's but that was turned down by the Scottish Office in 1990 without a public inquiry, and for the first time the Government was unambiguous about the importance of the Cairngorms landscape. A 'Save the Cairngorms' campaign mounted by conservationists proved an articulate and influential exercise, and the Secretary of State for Scotland received 7,120 objections to the new Lurcher's proposals, and 135 letters in support.

In one sense, devastation of the mountain was quite literally built into the development in 1960 when every damage limitation option – transport which did not require roads, for example, or a buses-only road, or higher, more expensive standards of construction – was rejected. If nothing else, at least the ski-developers' determination to violate Lurcher's finally proved to be the catalyst which brought the whole question of the Cairngorms management under much closer public scrutiny. If that scrutiny finally delivers a verdict on the landscape's behalf, it will be the first and last service which skiing will have accorded the Cairngorms.

Within a few months of the decision to reject the Lurcher's scheme, the Countryside Commission for Scotland published its much-vaunted report 'The Mountain Areas of Scotland' with the altogether predictable recommendation to create one of four national parks in the Cairngorms. Soon the Government was announcing a submission to UNESCO to have the Cairngorms designated a World Heritage Site and the formation of a working party to study the future management of the Cairngorms. Neither of these events is particularly significant in itself: national parks are a much rejected option in Scotland where very little enthusiasm can be found for importing the English and Welsh national park systems. Indeed Adam Watson, a commissioner himself, went so far as to dissociate himself publicly from the recommendations of the Countryside Commission for

Scotland – a critical blow to the credibility of the proposals. Britain's only other World Heritage Site are the islands of St Kilda, where so august a designation has not prevented expansion of a hilltop radar station, nor brought any improvement to the appalling impact of the Army base on a spell-binding landscape. Collectively, however, it may perhaps be said that all these proposed measures represent the first hint of changing priorities, of a slow awakening even in the Government to its responsibility towards landscape.

The last real opportunity to serve the landscape's cause was turned aside in 1954 when the boundaries of the Cairngorms National Nature Reserve were defined. Against the advice of outstanding naturalists such as Desmond Nethersole-Thompson, the Cairngorm-Ben Mac Dhui plateau was omitted from the Reserve, and so too was the shore of Loch Morlich. In this single thoughtless stroke two of the Cairngorms' richest wildlife habitats were rendered hopelessly vulnerable. Later extensions to the Reserve in 1963 and 1966, came too late to stop the rot which had already set in, and in any case the boundaries still shy well clear of Loch Morlich. The plateau has since been crushed underfoot by hordes of people who take advantage of the ski-tows' year-round operation to hitch a lift to four thousand feet. The loch, once a haven for waders, shielded from even the new ski road by a wild belt of unbroken woodland, has been sacrificed to the demands of tourism. Its foreshore, once a necklace of untrampled wild places, haunt of discreet greenshanks, is now hamstrung with car parks, picnic places, bulldozed roads, loud with tourism's clamour, bereft of greenshanks and all their wader tribe. Nethersole-Thompson and Adam Watson commented in their classic natural history book *The Cairngorms*: 'Planners in many countries forbid developments between a public road and an interesting nearby shoreline, but this excellent principle has been unashamedly ignored here, even though the loch is in a forest park where one would expect special care.'

So Cairngorm and its approaches today are massively defaced. Old eroded ski roads still scar its flanks, the main access road with its vast car and coach parks tiered high on the mountain, ugly buildings, miles of snow fencing, miles more of eroded paths, ski-tows and their pylons, debris, spoil heaps, litter – all these are part of the disfiguring conspiracy. The Cairngorm Chairlift Company's insistence on running the tows and lifts through the summer for purely commercial reasons deposits thousands of often ill-prepared, ill-equipped people on to the summit plateau (the Countryside Commission for Scotland memorably describes them in all seriousness as 'the non-active visitor') and the land simply withers under such artificial pressures.

Climbers and walkers use the chairlift too. Webs of new paths are ground into the frail soil and cairns litter the paths. There are demands for new bridges and other crutches for the incompetent. Organised mass events traipse over the mountains, never suspecting that such a thing as the spirit of the wilderness could ever draw breath here.

The Glen More road running east from Aviemore to the ski slopes has eased the passage of all these infiltrations. It is an often unflattering avenue of fast-buck developments latching on to every fad of the leisure and tourist business, a procession of roadside signs pronouncing their wares. Only a tiny minority of Glen More's developments show that any thought has been given to the landscape. For most of its length the road is an unforgivable denial of the worth of its surroundings, a monument to the worst excesses of bad forestry, uncaring tourism and downhill skiing. Yet just a few decades ago it was merely a forest track beyond Coylumbridge. The Scottish Mountaineering Club Guide to the Cairngorms of the late 1920s and early 1930s (the first years of the Forestry Commission's ownership of Glen More) paints a picture which is almost idyllic by comparison, idyllic but haunted:

> Glen More is said . . . to be haunted by a giant spectre, the Lamh-deirg (red or gory hand) who offered battle to belated travellers through the woods. There are two driving roads to Glen More Lodge, one running direct from Coylumbridge to Loch Morlich and the other coming in from the north by the picturesque pass, the Slugan . . . The first is now almost impassable for vehicular traffic. The Slugan road is kept in good repair by the Forestry Commission but is closed against motor-driven vehicles. Horse-drawn vehicles and push cycles are allowed . . . The right of the Forestry Commission to discriminate between different kinds of vehicular traffic is challenged in some quarters . . .

Oh for a return to discrimination between different kinds of vehicular traffic! And, for that matter, for the occasional discouraging re-emergence of the bloody-handed one. There are many travellers along that road who might be swayed elsewhere by the threat of mortal combat! Affleck Gray, long-time student and chronicler of the Cairngorms legends, attributes to the 'Bodach Lamh Deirg' ('Old Man or Spectre of the Bloody Hand'), the further recommendation of some of the qualities of a thinking conservationist. 'He was a gigantic figure . . . clad in the full panoply of a Highland warrior. One hand was always dripping with blood . . . Despite his terrifying and bellicose attitude, there seems to have been a kind and humane streak in him, for he assumed the role of guardian of the wild creatures in the forest, and woe betide any hunter who trespassed too much in his domain.' The Bodach has kept all too low a profile these last three turbulent decades in the landscape's history. I have begun to fear for him. Perhaps he has been run over by a skiing coach.

In the Bodach's hey-day, his domain would have been an unbroken tract of the Caledonian pine forest, the natural native garb for much of Highland Scotland. Birch, hazel, juniper, rowan thrived there too, but it was the shape and the shade and the scent of the Scots pine which stamped the forest with its distinctions. They still distinguish almost every approach to the Cairngorms (Rothiemurchus means the Great Plain of the Firs) but you cannot contemplate any contemporary treatise on their status without also reading or hearing the words 'remnant', 'relict', 'extinct'. The Forestry Commission began hammering hefty nails into the coffin of the Glen More pines in the 1930s. Large areas were planted with cash crops – mostly exotic conifers such as sitka spruce and lodgepole pine. Although we are supposed to be more enlightened now, more sensitive to the needs of conservation, clear-felling and new planting still continues.

Meanwhile, the pines constrict and wither, their unbroken lineage back through ten thousand years to the last Ice Age dismissed. Threats to the pinewoods are not new. That dark, benevolent plaid so rich in wildlife, sanctuary of bear and lynx and beaver and wolf in earlier centuries, has been exploited by many human eras. Centuries of felling to meet the demands of industry in the south, to accommodate first sheep and then deer in the aftermath of the Highland Clearances, to fuel the engines of destruction in two world wars – all these demands have brought the forests to their knees, dragged them down to the rim of extinction. The brutality of the deer-forest regime, which still pervades much of the Cairngorms, has slaughtered the pines. The economics of the sporting estates demand high numbers of deer, but there are more than the land can stand. The grazing – and consequently the quality of the deer – is impoverished, the land exhausted. In the eastern Cairngorms particularly, in Glen Derry, Glen Quoich, Glen Dee, and Glen Lui, the deer have the pines by the throat. The only substantial tracts of trees fenced off against their predations are the commercial plantations, almost inevitably of spruce. Yet it has been demonstrated again and again that all the native woodlands need are a fence or fewer deer or both.

A conference at Inverness in 1990 was told that red deer occupied three million of Scotland's seven million acres and were 'overgrazing, trampling and eroding the uplands'. In the previous twenty-five years, red deer numbers had doubled to 300,000, but the result of absentee landowners failing to effect a winter cull of hinds is that there is a population imbalance of well over 200,000 hinds to as few as 86,000 stags. The only solution is a huge cull of hinds, perhaps 50,000, perhaps many more, but the Red Deer Commission says that could take several years. Nevertheless, that is the scale of the problem, and the scale of the only kind of solution which will result in any significant change for the better in the health of the landscape. The Nature Conservancy Council has achieved startling resurrections of birchwoods at Inshriach on the River Feshie by fencing, and on a grander scale at Creag Meagaidh to the south-west of the Cairngorms by shooting or catching live huge numbers of red deer.

These remain isolated achievements, however, costing a great deal of money and demanding sustained commitment. Most landowners eye them with suspicion or outright hostility, and the lessons go largely unheeded. The pinewoods still wither a little more each year, yet in the best of the pinewood remnants, particularly in Rothiemurchus, there are arguably more elements of pure wilderness than anywhere else in Britain. The most quoted anthem to these trees was written in 1953 by foresters Steven and Carlisle, authors of *The Caledonian Pinewoods of Scotland*, still today the definitive assessment of the forests' worth. 'To stand in them,' they wrote, 'is to feel the past.'

Stand in them, then, and know that when you do, these same trees were brushed by wolf and Jacobite, doomed species both of eighteenth-century Scotland. Stand in them and feel the past and fear for the future. If the pinewoods go the way of the wolf, it will be an infinitely greater felony, because man has long since passed the day when he could say with any honesty that he never knew.

The changing philosophies of the sporting estates have also caused new disfigurations on the face of the wildest Cairngorms. The cynical fashion for bulldozed roads arose in the 1960s and shows no sign of fading. There are now thousands of miles of them in the greater Cairngorms area, ferrying shooters by Land-Rover to grouse moors and deer-stalking areas. Not even the Cairngorms National Nature Reserve is immune, and off-road vehicles are often driven far beyond the end of the tracks, far out over the plateau. Legislation to deal with the problem was fashioned by the Countryside Commission for Scotland and implemented in 1980, and has since become almost a showpiece for the futility of our efforts to safeguard landscape. The Act was supposed to require that planning approval from the Commission should be given before roads could be bulldozed within National Scenic Areas (the Commission's own highly subjective list of Scotland's most important landscapes), yet when it was brought to bear on two now infamous cases in Glen Ey and Glen Feshie, where roads were bulldozed without permission, both were granted 'retrospective planning permission' – two more blows inflicted on the sanctity of wilderness.

Then, in November 1990, Highland Regional Council's planning committee came to a remarkable decision. Glenfeshie Estate had extended an old bulldozed road by three hundred yards without planning permission and without consulting the council, doubtless assuming that the old retrospective planning permission trick would work here too. It did not; the council declined to give permission, and set about making an enforcement order to restore the ground to its wild state. Just three hundred yards, a scratch on the face of the land when the real problem is multiple lacerations, but at least it is a straw to clutch. Time will tell whether it is a precedent or an aberration.

The combined weight of tourism, some local authorities, and elements of the countryside 'establishment' has inflicted other bruisings. The tourist industry relentlessly promotes the Cairngorms and equates success with ever-increasing visitor statistics, without ever questioning either the quality of the tourist's experience or the fact that such a policy can only diminish, dilute and demean the landscape which is flaunted so glossily. The Cairngorms cannot handle more people, any more than the pinewoods can handle more deer. The evidence of a withering landscape is irrefutable. Local authorities all too often view tourism only in terms of jobs, and it seems no price is too high to pay for them. Tourism is, regrettably, a vital part of the Highland economy – regrettably because it is an unexacting host and a fickle provider. At the core of even its own definition of success, however, is a beautiful landscape. When that beauty is scarred beyond recovery, and the Cairngorms have already begun to lurch towards that condition, then tourism too will suffer.

The problem was confronted sixty years ago by Wendy Wood, patriot, poet, painter, champion of her heritage, and author of a lovingly observed book called *The Secret of Spey*. She wrote:

> Loch an Eilein is the show-place of Rothiemurchus. It is strange that praise and appreciation should be capable of spoiling a place as it may spoil a person. A loch cannot look superior and an island cannot preen itself; and yet Loch an Eilein . . . is spoiled by popularity . . .
>
> Country people, a horse, even a horse and cart, do not disturb the unity of Loch an Eilein, but anything in the shape of a car, whether it be the grocer's van or a Rolls Royce, is as incongruous as a bowler or a lum hat worn in conjunction with a kilt. Town shoes, perched precariously among the roots of the ancient trees that edge the water, fill me with a sense of shame. I can find no logical reason why people should not come in cars . . . but at the sight of them I hastily retire, like the osprey ever driven to farther retreats. [The ruined castle on Loch an Eilein's island was once famous for its osprey eyrie.]
>
> They are not rowdies who come to Loch an Eilein, they do not leave peel and papers about, but they do scatter the litter of their minds. 'Awfully jollies' and 'dashed fines' and 'stunnings' and 'by joves' lie about in the air, more conspicuously than cigarette-ends on the turf . . .

What would she make of Loch an Eilein today? The estate has built a car park and charges city centre prices for its use. On a busy day there may be sixty or seventy cars left there at any one time and the day's turnover will number hundreds. The shoreline vegetation has been obliterated. What began modestly as a discreet nature trail round the loch is now almost devoid of nature. A visitor centre sells craft produce, postcards and sweets, and yes, the visitors do leave peel and wrapping papers lying about, as well as cans and much else besides. Once a broken frisbee bearing the words 'water sports' floated in the shallows for weeks, a small symbolic monument to tourism's rubbishing of the landscape.

The most persistent complaint among visitors to the centre these days is over the mountain bikes which whoop gaudily round the lochside path. 'Can't the estate do something about the number of mountain bikes?' they ask. It can and it does. It hires them out to tourists.

Spoiled by its own popularity, Loch an Eilein has now finally been wrecked by tourist promotion, by a relentless industry which gives no thought to the consequences of its worst excesses. The place has more people than it can bear, yet the promotion of Loch an Eilein is unremitting and unrepentant. In that sense, it is a metaphor for the whole of the Cairngorms. It was persecution, not tourism, which drove the ospreys from the loch at the turn of the century, but it is noticeable that since they recolonised Strathspey they have shied well clear of their old breeding ground.

Yet Loch an Eilein is still beautiful, still 'lying behind birch-clad Ord Ban, reflecting the big hills of the east, encircled with dark fir, dressed with water lilies and bejewelled with a castled island' as Wendy Wood has it, but its beauty demands the averting of your eyes from its wounds and its tarnishings. If the promotion ceased and the car park were closed, the wounds would heal, the beauty would be utterly restored, and even nature would put in a reappearance. I cannot believe that the fact that many people find pleasure in their surroundings there, as they are, can justify what Loch an Eilein has become. The same might be said of the entire Cairngorms range.

Of course, it could have been so much worse. Watson and Nethersole-Thompson's book lists a breathtaking catalogue of development proposals which failed to materialise. A number of these still resurface from time to time among the private and public ambitions of vested interests. They include new tarmac roads up Glen Quoich to Beinn a Bhuird for skiing; a main road from Linn of Dee through Glen Feshie to Kingussie; a new road through Abernethy Forest and the Revoan Pass to Cairngorm, again for skiing purposes; a new road from Tomintoul to Crathie with spurs for skiing on Ben Avon; persistent calls for a road through the Lairig Ghru (but not so far as part of any serious development proposal); an eight-hundred-bed mountain village and church on Cairngorm; an airstrip in Glen Quoich; helicopter shuttles to take skiers to the summits; a Grampian Way official footpath through the Lairig Ghru; draining the Insh Marshes to create marginal farmland – and many more such schemes.

All these ideas represent somebody's short-term ambitions for the mountain landscape of the Cairngorms. The controversies have raged for forty years, and they rage now with greater intensity than ever. The mountains, now recognised for their international significance, are still no better protected.

All these debates have erupted against the background of an ominous prevailing climate within some of our countryside bureaucracies. It evaluates the landscape in terms of what people can get out of it, a 'recreation resource' in bureaucratspeak; visitors are 'countryside users'. Words like 'heritage' and 'resource' are bandied with reckless interchangeability. The result is to devalue, at least psychologically, the importance of the landscape, to trivialise people's experiences within it, and to diminish the sense of responsibility which people should feel towards landscape. All that is an insidious poison for wildness.

The Cairngorms landscape is unquestionably 'heritage' – Highland heritage, Scottish heritage, British heritage, European heritage. The idea that it exists solely, however, as a 'resource' to be exploited is a stupendous arrogance on the part of the exploiters and their political and bureaucratic allies. The Cairngorms exist to be the Cairngorms, a mountain landscape nurturing its own indigenous habitats and their wildlife. The landscape matters first and last for its own sake. It owes us nothing, yet it offers immeasurable rewards to those who revere it. But in the Cairngorms, it becomes more difficult to revere (on

Cairngorm itself it has long been impossible) because the exploiters have hammered parts of the mountains into a degree of submission from which they may never recover.

Heathcote Williams wrote in his long poem *Whale Nation*:

> In the water, whales have become the dominant species,
> Though they allow the resources they use to renew themselves.

A wise and revering countryside user, the whale.

A paragraph in the Countryside Commission for Scotland's policy paper, *Westward Expansion of Skiing at Cairngorm*, reads:

> Some recreational groups will declare that the enjoyment of their activity will be affected by the westward expansion of alpine skiing. It is difficult to quantify such claims as they relate to preferences for space and solitude-seeking activities as against the more gregarious nature of downhill skiing. At present, there is an element of zoning westward from the existing ski-field, with decreasing numbers and intensity of use.

What hope is there for wildness as long as the debate centres on arguments like that? What hope for the fragility of that wildness? There *are* solutions to the problems which confront the Cairngorms landscape, ways by which *we* can allow the resources *we* use to renew themselves, but they are all drastic ones. They must be implemented quickly and sustained far beyond our own lifetimes. I have my own definitions of what these might be, but they should come later, so that they can be seen to have grown from the explorations, experiences and landscape intimacies which have shaped them.

I begin again where I paused, by the summer snowfields, these old snows which so epitomise that characteristic of the Cairngorms which is never considered in their management – Arctic-ness.

2

Listen to the Hills

THE OLD SNOW is a metaphor for the mountain. It has its river valleys and marshes in the sodden surroundings fed by its leaking meltwaters. It has its fringing forests in the alpine plants and mosses which flourish in its shadow and by its grace. It has its corries in the scooping sculptures of heat and rain. It has its plateau where you can step from rock on to snow and know the ground no less firm beneath your feet. It has its bedrock in the oldest snows at its heart which may never melt, where even this sun has not won through.

The old snow has broken the back of the heatwave. It will survive now to feel the first cool fingerprints of the new season's snows, perhaps a month from now, perhaps a week. There is nothing new or even particularly rare about early September snows in the high Cairngorms. Cameron McNeish, broadcaster, editor of a climbing magazine and friend, lives addictively in the shadow of these mountains. When he was snowed on in August 1987, it completed his snow calendar, because until then he had known snow on these mountains only during the other eleven months of the year. As I write, I am still two summer months short – July and August – but somewhere in every Cairngorms season it will soon be winter again. In August 1989, a girl aged eight died of hypothermia near Lurcher's Gully in conditions described by the mountain rescue team as 'wintry'. Here, of all our landscapes, is winter's kingdom.

These old snows give pause for thought – how old? Seton Gordon, whose matchless contribution to the literature of the Cairngorms spanned more than sixty years, wrote in 1925 that the snowfield of the Garbh Coire on Braeriach has 'never within living memory been known to disappear'. Here, before my own eyes, is evidence of the same phenomenon. A rare eight-week high summer heatwave, yet the snow has survived it. Is there a parcel of snow crystals at the heart of this old wedge which has rested intact and unmoved through countless summers, so that it has won the snow tribe's rarest accolade of great old age? Is this soiled outer garment of the snow where I now stand itself a snow of older winters than the one which more or less gave up the ghost three-quarters of the way through last spring?

Such is the pace of change when the landscape is permitted to act of its own accord that a piece of snow, of all ephemeral things, may never melt. Is that melted snow which glistens darkly down the red granite rockface, or is it the shed symbolic blood of the mountain's pierced heart?

For the Cairngorms, like the old snows, dwindle and diminish in my eyes. This heatwave will end soon – heatwaves in the Cairngorms almost always end soon – and the old snow will be spared for three seasons more, perhaps three years more, perhaps three centuries, but somewhere in the mountain's story there may come a greater heatwave or turbulent seasons of long, unhinging rains, or both, and these will conspire to wipe the oldest snows from the hill. Or perhaps the climate will cool a degree or two and win back permanent snowfields across all the great corries. I believe the wildness of the Cairngorms, the total mountain, is as perilously poised.

It is the uniqueness of the Cairngorms that many people seem to miss, probably because it is not particularly obvious at first glance. Besides, conservationists have been all too free with the trite labelling of landscapes as 'the last great wilderness', and most of them are also labelled 'unique'. But these are not words which should be stitched into every objection to every other forestry or fish farming development in the land, because their true meaning in a landscape context carries a quite awesome significance. In the Cairngorms, they resound with that ring of truth.

There are shades of wilderness from hints and tastes to brutal confrontations all across the Cairngorms massif – on the plateau, in the remoter corries and in the innermost fastnesses and highest rock-limpeting extremities of the pinewoods – which can imbue or dominate utterly a human spirit; there are uniquenesses of landform, wildlife, climate. All these can elevate the landscape, to dignify, to humble even people. All these *do* conspire to accord the landscape its unique Arctic-ness. It is why so many unwary people die here, and it is why the snow buntings – my white sparrows of Ben Mac Dhui – do not.

The snow buntings have stayed on with the summer snow, scattering their own sparse and free-wheeling four-season blizzard about the highest rocks. These birds are literally in their element here, so loyal to it that they defect northwards only in rare and protracted milder eras. Snow buntings have a way of breaking down barriers between man and wilderness among those few who climb to learn their secrets and their high-flown ways. Chief among these, a giant among birdmen, Desmond Nethersole-Thompson wrote of individual birds he got to know 'almost like people'. I cannot see these mountains, from whatever distance, or even encounter the word 'Cairngorms' in print or in speech without being at least subconsciously aware of the bunting ballet, without hearing in my mind's ear that small shifting symphony of grace notes and rock leviathans.

The converse is also true, so that wherever I encounter snow buntings they evoke the Cairngorms landscape. The most bizarre experience of that thought process – in St Kilda of all places – revealed a strength of feeling in me for the Cairngorms and their small bird symbol which caught me unawares, because until that moment I had never seriously tried to assess it. One of St Kilda's hodden, sodden grey days bore down on Village Bay shuttering out all sights, all sounds. The morose mood of my plod through low cloud, across a watershed to Gleann Mor, was eerily lightened by a sudden snatch of that old familiar fruity trill. A cock snow bunting – a real St Kilda rarity, though it is the kind of place where almost anything can turn up – was rooting in the mosses of the watershed, and at the sight and sound of it my wandering unfocused mind was flooded almost unbearably with images of those mountains I have known and loved best for longest. For as long as I watched the birds, the turmoil of landscapes cartwheeled around my mind. Abruptly it perched on a rock, flung me a snatch of song, then was gone, heading east aboard the ocean wind.

I stepped as suddenly from the clingfilm of the clouds – the sea shouted wildly up from the mouth of the glen, Soay's island hunchback slumped across a corner of the horizon, and the first great skua of Gleann Mor lined up a bombing run on my head. I was unequivocally back in St Kilda. A shutter had fallen on the snow bunting and the Cairngorms, and it was not until much later that I grappled with the significance of the hour.

St Kilda is the most compelling of islands, its isolation and ocean grandeur creating such a pervasive introspection that even the rare skyline emergence of the Western Isles forty miles to the east is an irrelevance. I was hooked, enthralled, a willing conscript to that introspection's marshalled forces. I was not looking for mental escape routes, yet the snow bunting had breached even St Kilda's defences and scattered something of the granite dust of that far land-locked plateau about the sea-crazed rocks. Perhaps the bird's startling inter-vention in an off-guard moment, with St Kilda's allure at its bleariest ebb, simply evoked the landscape antithesis of the islands – St Kilda's scale is a tumult of cramped verticals, the Cairngorms' an immensity of horizontals – so that the mind so ocean-bewitched fed fleetingly and fiercely on its oldest mountain preference. Perhaps, but I think that it goes deeper than that. I think it boils down to a kinship with the land, a sensitivity to its rhythms which is almost exclusively the prerogative of earlier eras than our own. Yet I have already witnessed at first hand something of what is still possible from writer and friend of the wild, Mike Tomkies, who won a closeness to the animal state that few of us could ever achieve, or would ever care to achieve. For the St Kildans such an awareness of their wild world was not choice but necessity, and even now, sixty years after its evacuation, there is much tangible evidence of their way of life. I admired and marvelled, and yes, envied, and perhaps not surprisingly I clutched at the straw unwittingly proffered by the snow bunting – I fell back momentarily on that wild landscape to which I have come closest. Here, in the Cairngorms' benevolent midst, I am most at ease with my life and nature's.

There is one good reason why that should be so. From my first stubbled stumblings in a field beside my childhood home on the edge of Dundee, the Cairngorms lay on the ultimate horizon of the hill-going tradition into which I was mercifully born. But it was the douce profiles of the Sidlaw Hills which infiltrated my youngest awareness of landscape. They beckoned from the top of the field; I went gleefully north on two unsteady wheels with no thought of the higher northern hills of the Angus Glens and the whitened horizon smudgings of unguessable mountains beyond. The Sidlaws were hills enough, and I grew into them gladly through all their seasons and a handful of young years, the apprentice years in which hillcraft is honed instinctively. Every lark's nest and curlew cry dazzled the senses, and a glimpse of soft-shoe roebuck was a conversation piece for a week.

One autumn day while I sunned myself on lowly Craigowl, summit of the Sidlaws, I watched a storm drag darkly across the Angus Glens, saw Dreish and Mayar, those round-shouldered over-lords of Glen Clova, suddenly doff their cloak of storms to emerge whitely irresistible. The horizon beyond was lost in an altogether more ferocious storm, and I became aware in that autumn instant of the relative scale of hills and mountains, and began to guess at their relative dangers and rewards.

I went in time to Dreish and Mayar and peered north again to what was now a mountain horizon without, it seemed, any northern limit, a winter school of white whales, the Cairngorms of my geography class, the most statistically impressive place in my school curriculum. At my back, the Sidlaws which once loomed so large in the north now folded calmly into the south. I remember waving to them as I turned to prowl among my new-found native hills. I have waved to landscapes I love ever since. Always, then, there would be an appreciative eye on the Sidlaws, a speculative eye on the Cairngorms, until, osprey-like, I went beyond the apprentice lands and kicked further north than I had ever climbed to taste the total mountain.

I do not say that this is the only way to go to the Cairngorms, although I do think that it may be the best. I acknowledge my place in the tradition is luck; I am more grateful for that great good fortune than I can ever convey. I do say, however, that you cannot buy the landscape bond or strap it on like skis or crampons, for that is the fruit of the labours of years.

However you come into these mountains, you will arrive in your own good time on that highest bouldery thrust of the plateau's surface

1 The Northern Cairngorms and Lairig Ghru

2 Carn Eilrig and a sentinel pine

3   Red deer gather by a moorland lochan in the depths of winter

4   Roe deer fawn in Rothiemurchus pinewoods

5   The dramatic corkscrewing patterns of a dead Scots pine

6   Crested tit, one of the charmers of the pinewoods

7 Twinflower, a rarity
of the pinewoods,
photographed by
Fred Gordon

8 Spring birches and
pine at Loch an Eilein

which is the summit of Ben Mac Dhui at 4,296 feet, there to have your senses staggered by skies without limit; by land which flows away almost level, dips unguessably, but rises to level out again, the whole surface rock-studded and summer-sheened like the stretched skin of a vast toad. You could never call the Cairngorms beautiful. It is their grandeur which compels. On the throne of all that grandeur, a sparrow-sized snow bunting sings and drowns out the mountain wind.

The plateau is the place to be bird-staggered. Something absurdly-legged and downy-ragged scuttles away from under your boot. A bird you would swear is so young it should barely be able to stutter a step, takes to articulate wings. It is a signal for the rocks to explode. Twelve ptarmigan, the colour of summer screes (a kind of grey-gold-tawny-tending-to-pinkish-at-sunset), and betrayed by the nervousness of one straggly youth, scatter a handful of yards to settle and vanish as they land, the whole nature of the appearing-and-disappearing trick a mesmerising thing of seconds which lasts a year, or a lifetime. By the time the new snows have stowed away the old for another year, that same Judas bird will have grown and whitened and learned that discretionary valour is the better part of Arctic survival. Sit tight, be a rock, and learn to pray for the blinding of eagle eyes which trickery rarely fools.

It is a priceless lesson, for it is only given to nature to outwit nature. Because as a species we have distanced ourselves so far from nature's guidance, grown so deaf to her rhythms, we have long since lost the ability to outwit her in a landscape such as this. Instead, our presence is marked by the whittling away of wildness. I believe that wildness to be beyond price, I believe it matters for many reasons, but firstly because, in the words of George Mallory, Everest climber, it is there.

Walt Unsworth, whose book *Everest* is a handsome peak in the literature of that mountain, suggests there was something more to Mallory's immortalised and seemingly trite response to a press conference question:

Mallory seems to have acquired the habit of using the word 'there' to indicate anything which had a mystical quality. It occurs first in a letter which A.C. Benson wrote to him in 1911, urging him to read a certain book which achieved a high quality 'by being there'. And during the war, Mallory had written home describing the sight of men digging trenches and how he would like to be able to draw them like figures from Millet, only 'more there'. To him, the word *there* seems to have gained an all-embracing meaning for mystical feelings which he could not exactly put into words – and this certainly applied to the climbing of Everest.

I find parallels of a kind in my high summer on the Cairngorms plateau, dowsed with cooling bunting song. In winter you can catch snow buntings storm-tossed all up and down the east coast, or cat-napping on Arthur's Seat in the heart of Edinburgh, but a rare natural perspective drops into place when you encounter these sparse breeding leftovers of winter's hordes carolling across the roof of the land. You dawdle down through the pinewood at homing dusk with the clicking hiss of Scottish crossbills, the fizzing of crested tits, the startling clatter of capercaillie and the mooching deer for company (for deer in appropriate numbers also belong). It all matters to me, and to thousands of others, not just because of its unbroken chain stretching back to the Ice, not just because it can lay genuine claim to uniqueness. It matters most because it is, in every sense, there.

If you will say your piece about the Cairngorms, you should first let the mountains say theirs. For that you must put your ear to the ground, be still, and listen to the hills. They remain (bar the summit slum of Ben Nevis) the highest wildest thrust of the Highlands. It is because I have listened to these hills for more than twenty years (and to the lesser hills of the tradition for ten more before that) that in this hour of the landscape's need I climb again to say my piece.

3

River Deep, Mountain High

THE RIVER SPEY never breaches the Cairngorms' mountain heartland, but it drinks deeply there, summoning burns and rivers to the common cause of its seaward crusade. It is, even more than the Dee, which is born almost in Braeriach's summit rocks, a river spellbound by the mountains. To board the Spey's wide lingering strath at Newtonmore, and, like the goldeneye, saunter its north-eastering passage, is to acclimatise thoughtfully to this mountain land. As you glance eastwards, the mountains materialise with distant, low-profile discretion. Surely these are not the feared and fearsome Cairngorms? They look like anyone's doorstep hills anywhere. How many people have died in rash response to that first crude assessment?

The Spey, coiling demurely through the commanding flatness of the Insh Marshes, is playing games. It is only when you reach Aviemore that the Cairngorms suddenly become startlingly convincing, unleashing the mighty mountain profiles which crowd down on the tumultuous triangular dimensions of the Lairig Ghru, the prima donna of all the Highlands' mountain passes. Before you have set foot on the mountains you should have learned the folly of first impressions if you have heeded the river's lesson. The Cairngorms beckon you through wide portals, then, having lured you within, close the door on the possibility of indifference.

The Dee is a less subtle tutor, a native element of the highest Cairngorms. It hurtles the mountains' heart-blood over the headwall of the Garbh Coire's vast rock amphitheatre, and pulses its own foaming artery eastwards with all possible haste. To pursue the Dee upstream from the Linn of Dee near Braemar is to be thrust headlong into the mountains' innermost (and almost uppermost) sanctum. The first time is a jarring, monumental journey. The second time merely astonishes because the memory of the first holds good.

I have long inclined towards the Spey. It has always seemed the front door approach to the mountains, a wide-horizoned, open-palmed landscape rather than the clenched fist of the uncompromising Dee. It is also the baptismal font of these mountains. They are more properly the Monadh Ruadh, the red mountains, named on Speyside to distinguish them from the Monadh Liath, the grey mountains, which range down the Spey's western flank. It is a Speyside summit – Cairngorm – which supplanted the Monadh Ruadh by being crudely pluralised and anglicised into the less than apt Blue Hills.

Strathspey also harbours wildlife riches and a diversity of habitats to which the east cannot lay claim, and in the Insh Marshes and the Caledonian pinewoods of Rothiemurchus and Abernethy are stored fascinations of which I never tire. I do not decry the eastern Cairngorms, which, spared the distractions and wounds of skiing and the Spey's over-zealous tourism, offer many compensations and command the loyalties of legions of Deeside addicts. I stravaig the eastern glens gladly – Quoich, Derry, Lui and Dee – and relish their contrast, but if I linger longest in Strathspey it is simply because it is where my instincts linger fondest.

Winter became uncharacteristically sluggish, an ill-tempered foul-mouthed thing which ran cold and wet before big squalls and dark noons like truculent sheep before a novice collie. For days the sodden winds snapped at the heels of the land. The Spey rose and rose, fanning far out across the Insh Marshes. A cock hen harrier sat on a favourite fencepost for hours, surrounded by water, with only his own unaccustomed reflection and a smatter of prospecting whooper swans for company. I suffered a week of it with no more than fleeting forays from the typewriter, dreaming of the Dee charging darkly from its rock womb, a new-born thunderer. I became as frayed as the weather, until in one pale-skied respite I wandered out in a state of mild desperation to a stretch of the Spey where the banks still held good and patches of soft sand still showed among the bankside roots of alder and willow and birch, and the air was mild and sweet.

The place bristled with robinsong, although it was only mid-January, and flocks of long-tailed tits rolled through the twiggy crowns of fieldside trees like squeaky airborne puffballs. There is no acrobatic feat beyond them, no pose too precarious, no impossible demands of landing and take-off. I would prescribe them by the gardenful for depressives, for to watch them is to feel happy.

Now there's a feebly human perspective for you! A winter flock of long-tailed tits is one of nature's prettiest illusions. The birds are handsomely pied and patterned black and white, irresistibly garnished with a lance-corporal stripe of liquorice allsort pink across their backs, a paler blush of the same colour to their bellies. But that decorous tail which so embellishes the ballet of their flight and assists their agility also causes inordinate heat loss for such tiny birds. In a hard winter they simply do not generate enough heat to live, and in the worst of it they can fail to live in their thousands, and take years to recover as a species. I have seen them packed together in a winter evening roost as close as semi-quavers, adjusting the formation on occasions to accommodate the outside birds in the middle of the line, this I assume a way of sharing the meagre ration of heat.

I had put a quiet mile of riverbank behind me with nothing more for company than a desultory squabble of rooks and jackdaws, nothing more than indistinctly old might-have-been otter tracks in the sand patches, when I found a no-question-about-it fish skeleton with the intact head and accusing eye – the nearest thing to a ghost in wildlife that I have ever seen.

So now – it happens so often within the force-field of the Cairngorms – the most casual of strolls had acquired a preoccupation, and I bent my head to the otter spoor. The tracks freshened upstream, sharp-clawed and new, discernible only where the sand lingered in fragments of the riverbank anything between a dozen and a hundred yards apart. Here were pages torn from the diary of the night and the dawn, thrown to the wind and impaled on the roots and the brambles and the rotting fences of the riverbank, to be read and decoded by anyone with seeing eyes and an inclination towards the everyday trivia of a prospecting otter.

I had read of a single beast working the tree roots where the river hissed darkly through their midst, taking to the mainstream to overcome major obstacles rather than the bankside path with its man-stench. Always, however, the otter came back to the next clear stretch of bank to scribble in the sand, perhaps to trouble the dawn roost of the goldeneyes which cruise the winter river, perhaps to find a day roost of its own under the roots.

The rooks dribbled noisily back and forward across the river's sky in a kind of clattering dirge which I began uncharitably to find irksome. Any big river like the Spey exerts calming influences if you watch it uncoil at close quarters, a fine blend of swift efficiency in the mainstream execution of its self-appointed task and slack water repleteness about the small bays and trees of the banks. The rooks gatecrashed all that like drunks at a party. I threw them one more grudging glance of the glasses, and as I followed them upriver they became shrunken silhouettes against the sudden and monstrous unveiling of the Cairngorms massif.

The mountains had been missing for days, lost in their own misery of storms. They re-emerged now, snow-stained and gale-tormented to impress again on the riverbank dawdler that this is a mighty river, even by Scotland's standards. Among these waters at my feet were the nursery gleanings of the Beanaidh Bheag, 3,500 feet up in Coire Beanaidh of Braeriach. Now that same corrie frowned down out of its high cloud crown across the miles of Strathspey. The Cairngorms have a far-flung influence which sometimes startles with a glance or a shaft of misplaced mountain wind, sometimes with a slow, seeping psychology. The otter knows it, foraging way up the mountain burns, crossing high watersheds, threading back to the highway river in an easy night's march.

My Speyside otter's tracks failed to re-emerge from the next unbroken colony of riverbank roots, so I returned, Poirot-like, to examine in detail the last evidence – and found none, un-Poirot-like. There was a clear line of tracks across two yards of sand from water to tree, then nothing. I considered the unlikely possibility that the otter was holed up for the day under the roots, that if I waited two more

38

hours I might see him emerge in the dusk. I might equally possibly not see him, even if he was there in the first place. I scribbled a note to myself to check the place again a few days later.

On the journey back downstream I realised that my afternoon had been deaved not by one hell-raising party of rooks but by a steady flow of them, a dozen at a time. It had been a reasonable assumption that the same wheeling birds were keeping erratic pace with me as I walked south, but now, walking north, I watched band after band of them flying querulously up out of the northern fields, homing in on an upstream roost. I saw too what I had missed when I found the fish which put me on the otter trail – a blatant, musky otter spraint on a wide, flat grassy projection of the bank, as conspicuous now as the fish itself. I then began to wonder if I *had* missed it the first time. It did seem very fresh. I began to wonder who had been following whom.

I returned to my typewriter through a wide swathe of Strathspey, cheered by the river, gladdened by the late afternoon light on *ad hoc* congregations of birches, buoyed by the windings through those hard-wrought farms which subside imperceptibly into the pinewoods of Abernethy. By the last of the farms, I frowned at what seemed in that faltering light to be a haphazardly worked black field. It looked as though the ploughman had gone straight out from the pub on a Satur-day night and ploughed through the night until he had sobered up, realised the folly of what he was about and retired with the job half finished. I reached for the glasses, and found all that afternoon's rooks and jackdaws assembled in a single field, upwards of two thousand birds. The song of that field carried on the wind was like a chorale for massed Chicago gangsters. It was, I think, the most cheerfully discord-ant event I ever attended. I listened until the air grew cold and the field grew dark. Still the birds drifted down from the north, the pack reshuffling as each new windfall added a jaunty descant to the main theme. Every bird's head was turned to the south, an ill-disciplined army on winter's parade ground. We thole our winters the best way we know how. Some of us are just louder than others.

January ebbed cold and coarse-crackling with the determination of iron fists on the thrapple of the land. After ten days it began to snow lightly, small driftings across the low sun as it arced down towards the roadside pines which screen the high fields and their friendly-familiar cottage. Sometimes the wind found a way through to kick small puffballs of snow along the track, or irritate the birch roots with hissing hornpipes. The stubbled fields beyond the cottage took on the air of an unmade bed of nails. I rang the cottage bell, pushed the door and called a greeting, but only the geese in the yard called back, so I turned to find a sheltered nook and cast an eye on the day.

The fields and fences thrummed with small bird life, falling on the cottage and its near neighbour for their liberal bird-table feasts. Hundreds sat in the cottage trees at any one time, flew to feed and back to perch, conserving energies for the next bird-table flight. Hundreds more speculated among the stubble, while the hunter birds, who know this cottage as well as the tits and the thrushes and the finches, marked the small bird commotions, and prepared to move in.

I caught the female buzzard's long dark glide from the high trees above the road to a big birch by the lower fields where she perched. From my own perch on the higher ground, we were almost level with each other, and close enough for me to see through the glasses her involuntary blink as a snowflake struck one yellow eye. She perched erect with her back to me, watched side-headed, thick-necked, broad-shouldered, square-tailed, like a compacted eagle. Her huge wing feathers where the snow glistened whitely, then wetly, were folded across her back in a perfect heart-shaped shield, a rich dark brown, the colour of well-seasoned oak. Her head turned and angled sideways and upwards as the long mewed cry of her mate sounded above and behind me. As her head moved, I saw clearly the snow touch and melt, touch and melt as the frail sun lit her new posture. She shuddered then, and heaved her feathers into a huge eagle bulk, reassembled herself, turned on her perch to present her paler chest, leaned out, kicked at the tree, and with slow dark-and-tawny strides came low across the stubble towards me, flying as though the snow was bearing her down. But she saw through my stillness and with a visible change of attitude wheeled and climbed in one subtle manoeuvre of her wings. With fan and flap and fluidity, they thrust aside the snow. Her tail rocked and spread and played the wind with uncanny assurance, discreetly complementing the wings' blatant power. Yet the buzzard was performing so comfortably within her limits that she gave me an under-the-wing assessing glance as she passed. She drove a cloud of small birds before her, but for the moment she too was retreating.

I followed her with the glasses, and as I dragged them across a dark belt of trees, going south, they caught then lost a slow and slim pale bird-blur going north. I relinquished the buzzard at that, fancying I knew what had crossed her path. I lowered the glasses, found a new panic of birds on the field's northern fringe, then, glasses raised again, homed in on the dark-white form of a hunting harrier, the gull-coloured male. Harriers are glider-shaped, all wings and tail and no torso, pencil slim in every limb, yet fashioning flights of stylish malevolence from seeming flimsiness.

He climbed to five feet to take the fence and its hedge rags, and then for the half hour that followed he cut and quartered the stubble, combing its bristles a notch above stalling speed, an inch or a foot above landing height. It was an inexorable, insinuating performance of menace, an undeniable technique, the pattern changing only in the sudden frenzy of pursuit – two strikes out of four – and the pause to feed from the reddening snows.

At the second strike, his mate, the dark brown 'ringtail', was suddenly low over another panic of finches which flicked into the air and bowled raggedly along like blown leaves in November bluster. The harriers shared meagre small bird spoils, rose a foot, two feet, to cast shadows of twice the menace about the field, to strike twice the terror into the winter-weary lives of the feeding flocks.

In all this time, the buzzards had perched and forayed and soared and huddled and hovered and caught nothing, but they are not really small bird predators, and perhaps they were just here for the sport of it, working off some earlier rabbiting ploy on the banks above the marsh.

I made a slow contouring crossing of the fields and found a wind-blunting cranny in the trees to put the half-hearted sun at my back (the better to see the harriers), but my careful working and worming to the edge of the trees unleashed a pair of sparrowhawks. Or perhaps they were ready to go anyway – needing a psychological shove, like a bather contemplating a cold pool – for their flight was headlong and lethal, hitting two finches in a tight wedge of fifty, not three yards and not half a second apart. I have never seen sparrow-hawks hunt in a pair like that before or since, nor had my foreground dissected by such contrasting predatory stylists as the hawks, the harriers and the buzzards (the hawks swift and slatey and small, round-winged, robust and blunt). Neither have I ever known two hours with so compelling a sense of wild theatre, in or out of Strathspey. Yet it was all the prize of a chance outing, a haphazard pursuit of a buzzard and a certain discretion in the watching.

At my last shivered glance before I backed into the trees and retreated along a roe's path, all six hook-beaks were in the air over the field. Two crows darted down at the female buzzard with black shouts, until the male dropped on them from above and clouted one out-manoeuvred tail. The buzzards rose and mewed – mirthfully it seemed – as a single black feather fell to the whitening earth. The hawks patrolled the middle heights, the hedges, the wood edges, herding small birds until they scattered or dived for cover and the hawks swooped or flew on. The harriers inched along on long wings, the ringtail the darker, larger shadow, the male as low and white as a rolled snowball. By the cottage, the bird-tables steadily emptied, the finches and their allies thickening the safest trees with their foliage. The snow grew as silently relentless as the harriers.

It was deep into February before I went back to the otter's riverbank. It had snowed for days on the high tops, and the previous day's low level fall still smothered much of the riverside fields and banks, and clung to the trees. It was in expectation of what I might read on that new diary page that I returned. There were no signs of otters, nothing more than a days-old spraint, old hints of tracks in the sand, and nothing new in the snow.

Flocks of tits still carolled and careered through the alders, working downstream, even across it. I was intrigued by their crossings, for the whole flock never seemed to cross at once, and always seemed to cross where the water ran quietest. The calm water clearly assisted communication. The contact calls ricocheted across the hundred yards of river like the shells of a demure gatling-gun. But where the river gossiped and clattered through the rocks, the flock held tight to a single shore, moved loosely within its own earshot. In winter, the importance of the flock is all. Come April, its survivors will pair off to contemplate the bizarre ritual of nest-building, for while others of the titmouse tribe throw a nest together in a hole, long-tails practise a deft architecture, an elaborate sphere fashioned from anything up to two thousand feathers. The brood crams the nest a dozen strong, and the first spilling of that instantly disciplined troupe into the world beyond the nest is one of the Speyside woodlands' delights. It strikes you again – to watch them is to feel happy. Yet just as winter takes a terrible toll, no small woodland bird is more devastated by predators in the spring. However wonderfully worked the long-tails' nest may be, it offers only warmth, and none of the defensive strength of a tree hole or a nesting-box.

I watched them skip out on the river air, chittering over to the far bank. I threw a thought after them: winter well.

Other eyes watched the tits trapeze from bank to bank, eyes set in twin monocles of gold which caught the late afternoon sun and blazed back. The head wore a burnish of bottle green, the cheeks blushed whitely, and in sudden awareness of my presence on the bank the spirit of the winter river – for as such have I come to think of the goldeneye – voiced its acknowledgment almost politely as if he was clearing his throat. The goldeneye is a diving duck, a cruiser of the quiet water, and flies with a rhythmic wheeze like a nicely tuned two-stroke engine which never contemplates missing a beat.

There are few stretches of the Spey around the Cairngorms where the drakes don't gather in threes and fours and half dozens. It is here too, in the trees of the strath, that they have begun to pay the landscape's wildness the ultimate compliment of establishing a small resident population, turning their backs on the ritual of spring migration to Scandinavia. It is still a slender toehold goldeneyes maintain on our springs and summers, but since the first breeding birds were found in the mid-1970s there has been a steady and discreet growth to a few dozen pairs. Ornithology holds its breath and does what it can to assist – nesting boxes in likely places for instance – excited at the prospect of a new breeding bird, while the holidaying hordes who traipse through this land are noticeably underwhelmed.

Ospreys are their ornithological yardstick, and nothing less than that bird's charismatic style will do. It is hard to imagine a million and more visitors coming to watch a duck.

The goldeneye demonstrates one more reason to value the greater Cairngorms area as a place apart which demands special consideration – so often wildlife in search of a new niche (or retreating into an old one) entrusts itself to the Cairngorms landscape. It has, uniquely, so much to offer.

My goldeneye began suddenly to go through his mating ritual, rearing up and throwing his head so far back over his tail that he seemed in danger of overbalancing backwards, each time with a kind of quacking snort like a cartoon duck. The performance was pre-sumably a gesture for the benefit of other drakes on the river – there were two well downstream and three more a hundred yards upstream – for there were no females in sight. He repeated the process several times, then seemed to re-establish an awareness of my presence, for he subsided by the far bank and began to feed. With every dive he showed vivid red legs, then he resurfaced and quacked quietly at me, then dived again.

Finally the upstream drakes squeaked overhead, he pirouetted and in four strides was in their wake. That left the river to me and a pair of energetically bellyflopping dippers, enthusiastically thirled to the rough water that the goldeneye and tits avoided.

I love dippersong. In every season and in any setting – trickling burn or grumbling Spey or high mountain cataract – the song is pitched just loud enough to carry above the sound of the water, a thin warbling burble that can last for minutes at a time, antidote to storm-bruised spirits.

I watched this Spey pair, the darkest shade of brown you wouldn't call black, white-bibbed, cock-tailed like a bloated wren, and won-dered at the flexibility of the species. I know a pair which nest under an old mill near Edinburgh. Their every nesting season flight takes them under or over a pedestrian footbridge much haunted by dog-walkers and stationary dipper-watchers like me, but none of that deflects their purpose or their breeding success. Then there was a warm day of late spring by the shore of Loch Coire an Lochain when that unmistakable sonata drifted up, as I thought, from the Beanaidh

44

Bheag, a few hundred feet below. Suddenly the singer himself confounded me by lipping over the last few yards of the corrie's burn and drenched that lochside — 3,300 feet up — with music. It was, I think, one of the sweetest moments I have shared in the Cairngorms.

Winter's song on the Insh Marshes is a pure, brassy embellishment to the wildness of the landscape, an anthem scored in the Arctic. It is borne south in the autumn on the wings of the herald birds, the changeling sons of princes, a wild tribe so steeped in Celtic, Norse and other mythologies and lore that it takes a brave naturalist or a singularly hard-headed one to dismiss them in biologically classifiable terms as *Cygnus cygnus* — swan swan.

Whooper swans have a presence. There is something in their lofty, conversational style, their measured elegance, their extra-sensory wariness and their perpetual restlessness which I find irresistible. If I had been the son of a Celtic prince rather than of a telephone engineer, I could have adjusted well to my duality. There are worse forms of schizophrenia than half-prince, half-whooper!

Nature has tumbled all her superlatives into swans. I have watched addictively the same pair of mute swans from early spring to late autumn; mooched tetchily north in September after the ospreys have gone south, seeking out the first whoopers from Iceland; trekked again and again along the old familiar routes to old whooper wintering haunts; diverted journeys for glimpses of aloof Bewicks.

There is, I think, real value to any wanderer of the wilds in marking such milestones of the seasons with conscious ritual or journey. It helps to restore a sense of that which is missing in most of us, a rhythmic awareness of nature's cycle. It does not matter whether you live in the lee of the Cairngorms or the Norfolk Broads or Clapham Common, for wherever there is evidence of nature there is a rhythm and rhyme and reason for the manner and pace of nature's bidding. Mike Tomkies caught it thus, in his book *A Last Wild Place*:

How inextricably intricate is the balance of nature, the way in which all in the natural world has grown to live with the seasons; at differing paces, to struggle, to thrive and finally submit. Only man has learned to create his own artificial city environments and overcome the worst of nature to his own benefit — although he has yet to overcome the worst in his own. He loses greatly, too, in no longer being a part, a close witness, of the pageantry of the seasons.

The whooper swans gather in the afternoons on a lochan in a corner of the marshes, untroubled, for all their newly-shed Arctic tranquillity, by the neighbouring railway, the old road beyond, and the new A9 beyond that. There is a lay-by on the new road, high above the lochan and well screened by a high bank thick with birches. It should be the perfect hide, but watching whooper swans undetected in anything other than the most artificial of circumstances is one of nature's trickier assignments.

I parked, climbed the bank, chose my tree screenings with painstaking care, and there, staring up at the glasses from two hundred yards away and fifty feet below were eighty white periscopes, every head alerted by the sentry birds, which divined my solitary arrival but had turned deaf ears and blind eyes on all the passing cacophony of Strathspey's commerce. Eighty is a large gathering for the lochan which looks crowded with half that number afloat. I retreated, primed the camera, noted the path of sun and wind, and fashioned a strategy to get close by way of a wide diversion across the marsh itself. The Insh Marshes are an accursed terrain for non-swans to traverse, laced with subtle treacheries – soft-bottomed pools which masquerade as tussocks, ankle-deep troughs which collapse under a boot to a depth of three feet, that kind of thing. With the sun at my back, the wind in my face, a scrappy willow screen to shield me, and the certainty of a soaking up to the knees at least, I made one hundred yards in twenty minutes. I slunk into the cover of the willows, explored three impassable routes, swore and stopped.

The swans were relaxed again. They fed, preened, dozed, muttered soft 'woopah!' parodies of their bugling flight and alarm calls. The willows grew to within thirty or forty yards of the lochan, less than that to the nearest birds which fed in the no-man's-land-and-water of the 'shore'. My aim, as it has been so many times before, was to settle in the edge of the willows so that I had unrestricted vision across the lochan but cast no discernible shape or silhouette on the backlit trees. Interesting theory. It was working well, too, and I stepped slow as a heron to within five yards of the edge of the willows, biting my tongue as another twig whipped the corner of an eye.

I was now absorbed in the swans, eavesdropping on their small talk, edging the last critical yards a silent pace at a time, a long pause, another pace. Every step felt the water to avoid an unseemly lurch into unsuspected depths. One ill-considered step now would wreck everything. Check the camera. Is it loaded? Of course it's loaded, oaf. The light on the lochan was a warm glow, the birds at their ease, their proximity putting a thudding tension in me. Four yards . . .

It is the ultimate irony of just such a situation that the closer you come to wildlife which is unsuspecting and at ease, the less relaxed you become yourself. It is the great salutory lesson of watching wildlife, that man cannot walk in its midst in any guise other than that of alien, interloper, threat. Three yards . . .

I did not see the reed buntings until they rose in a small chirring cloud of a dozen birds. They had been right above my head, the nearest within touching distance. They were not clear of the trees before the nearest swans uncoiled, scattered their 'woo-pah?' question marks on the air, marshalled the forces of retreat. Tension flickered through the flock like an eddy of wind across a still pool. As every up-ended feeding swan resurfaced, its voice swelled the chorus of concern. The water grew suddenly loud with a new emphatic ring about the birds' calls. Every bird crammed into the far corner of the lochan, wheeled to face the sun, the unmistakable prelude to take-off. For the moments of that wheeling manoeuvre the flock tightened into a thickening copse of twisting heads and necks, an exquisite confusion.

The foremost birds lost their nerve. With an unfurling of canopies of wings they thrashed out across the runway of the lochan and were airborne in a dozen strides, curving away low over the marshes. The others streamed behind them like the long glittering wake of a trawler. The air rang and rang with their trumpeting din. It was hardly the effect I had set out to achieve, but the sight and the sound of eighty swans wheeling across the slant of the sun, buoyant and brilliant against the dark cloth of the foothill forests, and the sun-swathed bulk of the Cairngorms overlording it all, is one which will live with me until I forget what swans and mountains look like.

The swans dipped down to the unseen river where it cuts its idling swathe far out across the flatlands, and disappeared as they landed, so that I was left suddenly with only the distant and disembodied chorus of their quietening throats for a souvenir of their spectacle. In fifteen minutes more there was neither sight nor sound. In such circumstances do you curse or bless the reed buntings?

There is an alternative to all this soaking stealth, a mountains-to-Mohammed approach to whooper-watching by which you can sometimes lure a small group of swans towards you. The technique simply involves imitating whooper calls from a position of reasonable concealment (a car is as good as anything if you can get it close enough to the water's edge). It is a vocabulary of three words, projected falsetto: 'woop!', 'woopah!' and 'woo-pah?' Woop is short and sweet, conversational; woopah is emphatic, the syllables falling roughly on soh and me in tonic solfa; woo-pah? has an interrogatory edge, rising from doh to lah. It helps if you listen a lot before you try it so that your woopah doesn't emerge like an emasculated cuckoo. Swans are unlikely to respond to cuckoo sounds. It is also worth looking over your shoulder from time to time. That way you avoid gathering a smirking audience of the entire local schoolbus, farmer, and policeman. But sometimes it works, it works!

Early March, and contradictions tumbled across Strathspey like ravens. The high tops had their biggest snowfall of the winter in the night, and greeted the morning with a white tranquillity which even down on the marshes dominated and lightened the land. Here, however, there was a spring in the step of the day, a new and still mildness. The river's goldeneye drakes sat on their glassy reflections, which conferred an ornamental air on them – painted birds, like, say, one of Tunnicliffe's oriental panels. Whoopers seemed to have massed suddenly, and I had counted three hundred birds in a long sweep down the west side of the marsh and up the east. That too is a portent of spring, although the very mention of the word before June in the lee of the Cairngorms is likely to induce the wrath of the snow gods, and invite the havoc of late frosts. Bare birches in May are not rare.

A giddy group of six buzzards were on the air, two of them free-falling and soaring in display flight, the others stacked up and circling like an airport landing queue. The neighbourhood rookery, frantic with their ribald construction industry's assembly and reassem-

bly of nests, despatched black ambassadors of acrimony to rough up
the buzzards. Such behaviour among all the crows is a compulsion of
unquestionable courage and questionable logic. The range of raptors
hereabouts – eagle, buzzard, osprey, goshawk, sparrowhawk, kestrel,
harrier, assorted owls – consumes a lot of useless crow energy. At best
a momentary discouragement is achieved, at worst the raking slash of
a retaliatory talon maims an over-zealous protestor. There is little
return for endeavour in mounting an attack on six buzzards when the
most lethal weapon in your armoury is your voice, but the stir around
the rookery is the first tangible commitment to the new season.

These are pivotal days of the wild year. The irresistible process of
light and renewal has begun, and even in winter's kingdom the forces
of spring are marshalled to breach such defences as are left vulnerable.
A little elevation goes a long way on the Insh Marshes. A birchy knoll
of fifty feet throws you half a world, miles wide, which lies
unsuspected beyond your gaze when you are down at water level. It is
a restless wild theatre, its stage thrumming at every season with a
fluctuating cast of principals and strolling players. On that morning of
early March, a small squadron of dayglo oystercatchers wheeled low
over the marsh, adding colour and clamour to the riverbank. A flock
of thirty lapwings flirted in and out of hesitant sunlight, new arrivals
too, making for the grasslands of the farms which flank the marsh's
east boundary, and where the fields still grow dark and loud with
geese. The harriers and hawks will eye the lapwings' arrival with
approval, for a slow and conspicuous flock is an easy target, and there
are few enough of these through the long Strathspey winter.

These birchwoods which climb sharply from the eastern fringes of
the Insh Marshes characterise almost all approaches to the
Cairngorms. Here they establish an instant perspective across the
marshes and put the role of the river in its place. They put their own
stubborn stamp on the land, and in their innermost recesses offer you
nothing but the depths of their own silvery kingdom. From the edge
of the marshes, however, they lure your eyes up the mountain
ramparts of Glen Feshie, an inexorable order of landscape whose rules
were laid down by the Ice Age.

When the Ice relented ten thousand years ago, the first trees to
thrive again were birches like these. It is no meagre memorial, a

49

Cairngorms birchwood. The one which bears more of the Ice's hall-marks than any other is a tract of Deeside, a handsome filamore about the waist and shoulders of Morrone above Braemar. The highest trees cower before the snow winds at more than two thousand feet. The wood's characteristics – stunted, misshapen trees, a dense understorey of juniper, a diversity of mini-habitats and an equally diverse range of alpine plants – are all more redolent of Scandinavia than Scotland, one more small symptom of the Arctic. The difference is that for this Arctic fragment to survive here, it must also survive a brutal deer-grazing regime.

I climbed the wood in early March, found almost at once a wide shelf of the hillside thronged with red deer, hugged the thickest trees to avoid alarming them, but put up a white hare from almost under my boot. That was all the notice of my presence which the deer needed. The deer marked its blatant dash across the dark land, and marked the source of its alarm. A small fringe group of hinds snorted disapproval and turned in a trotting easterly retreat, enough to bring the couched stag herd of three hundred to its feet and edge them slug-gishly eastward too. Their stiff-legged, high-headed gait rumbled quietly across the hill. An hour of light snow had dusted and dulled their coats. Now as they stood and ran, a flimsy sun darted among them, struck a glistening sheen on their flanks, lit the half-hearted snow with a soft glare. It was an unashamedly exciting spectacle, the stuff of the Scottish Highlands' unquenchable tourist appeal. It is also killing landscapes like these. The handsome culprits paused to stand again and throw long antlered gazes back across the hill at my accu-sation.

A fenced off acre or two at my back – a simple scientific experi-ment – is crammed with irrefutable evidence. The deer are banished from its sanctuary and the trees and the juniper and the moorland floor are thick and thriving. Outwith the fence, where the deer flourish, the trees are sparse, the juniper stunted, the moorland floor impoverished, the landscape architecture of the Ice Age as betrayed and degraded as slums. It would not be permitted in Georgian Edin-burgh; it should not happen in the midst of nature's masterpieces either.

I knelt by the hare's couch and felt its flattened grasses. They were warm and dry, although every surrounding shred of the moorland was snow-sodden, ice-cold. It was a long stillness I had interrupted.

The mountain hare whitens and darkens – like the ptarmigan – by spasmodic degrees as the seasons ebb and flow. It runs before the wind, keeps mostly to the leeward side of the hill, ranges with the weather from the highest adventures of the brown hare at around a thousand feet to the plateau three thousand feet higher. In the worst of the winter weather, it lies low often for hours, in couches like the one at my feet, or snow burrows. I considered such cultivated patience. How does time pass – in thought or thoughtlessness? Does the hare leap, ruled by instinct, at every encroaching footfall, or discriminate between, say, harmless roe and fox foe, classifying their approach into sounds and scents, responding accordingly? Are fox and wildcat adjudged lesser risks than eagle and buzzard which scour these skies, in which case does the hare tend hereabouts towards a wood such as this where eagles dare not but fox and wildcat might thrive? And what terrors does the most un-birchwood-like footfall of all – yours and mine – hold for the hare?

So often we write animal behaviour off as instinct. I tend towards the idea that as often as not they think things out for themselves. If the hare in its long winter stillnesses must respond one way or another to all the footfalls of the mountain birchwood, and all the silhouettes of its skies, as facts of everyday survival, a sophisticated degree of discrimination is perfectly plausible.

In my wanderings through that birchwood day to the open ground above, I saw thirty hares and startled a dozen of them, watched others spar their madcap 'boxing' rituals on the high ground (a vivid advertisement to the eagles, but always with the option at least of a fast downhill retreat into the trees). As I cleared the highest birchwood, I saw six hares lope easily uphill above me and stop precisely on the skyline where their whiteness was immediately rendered silhouette black. A fluke of the moment of my sightline stopped them in orderly single file, neatly spaced down the skyline, all six tall-eared and still, a frieze of Indian head-dresses on the brow of the hill. Then the leader dropped beneath the skyline, the others following in desultory indiscipline, their whiteness restored, the daft moment of imagery done. I watched them rummage down the hillside, then suddenly split and panic, a galvanised frenzy that left me gasping at its explosive energy. Two of the six took the steepening uphill slope at a gallop and disappeared into its murky heights. The others spilled downhill, deep into the sanctuary of the wood, but I fastened my glasses on to the nearest one and watched his headlong blur take a thousand feet of often precipitous and bouldery birchwood at an unrelenting gallop, saw him cross the road below (where white-furred corpses are no rarity) and bolt on down to the open ground by the River Dee itself. It was an astounding retreat, a thing of a handful of seconds, a *tour de force* of reckless agility over such a terrain.

A golden eagle appeared cruising the crags above the wood, low and slow over the land as a harrier, dipping a wing which wore the white badge of his tribal immaturity. He would know this for a good hare hill, know too that although the scattering retreat of the six had eluded him brief patience would create new opportunity, and there were two at least above him on the open ground, two which had shunned the birches and placed their faith in stillness and snow and the small drifting clouds of the summit..

I turned back down the wood in the path of the headlong hare, marvelled again at its downhill mastery over rocks, sudden bogs, dead bracken, fallen trees, pools, burns, ditches, tussocks. There had been not one faltering foot. I put up another hare then, watched it semi-circle below me to stop and stare, and in that moment of brief sun I sat by an aged birchwood veteran to stare back. We made what we could of each other's presence, cast an eye sideways at a roebuck which threatened to intrude (but he was downwind of me, and bounced back the way he had come with a sharp 'bow!' to an unseen follower) and finally had our concentration snapped by a close buzzard cry. The hare's ears shifted at that, and I almost sensed his growing discomfort at the suddenly compounded dangers of his position. Three buzzards hove into view working the edge of the shelf and its winds, on a line which would take them right over the hare. The hare, meanwhile, was pinned to the moor by the sunlight, as blatant as a rib of quartz. One by one, the buzzards sailed past, not thirty feet above; one by one they ignored the hare and its vulner-ability, guessing perhaps that before they could fall on him he would be deeper into the trees where it would take the wings of a particularly ambitious sparrowhawk or a goshawk to fashion effective pursuit. I was unconvinced, however, and as the buzzards wheeled and worked back upwind, I rose and put the impetus to flee into the hare's spring-heeled gait. The buzzards and I went our ways, hareless.

It is a cruel fate to be born a mountain hare. The hook-beaks are against you – eagle, buzzard, the slowly re-establishing goshawk; jaws are against you – fox, wildcat (pine marten and stoats will tackle the leverets); guns are against you – a hare drive can slaughter hundreds on a 'good' day; traffic is against you – a straight-line flight offers no resistance on today's roads. I am a fan – I delight in the explosion of a snowdrift into thirty scattering hares, in finding leverets (twice) on the plateau at well over three thousand feet, but I can't pretend such encounters have enlightened my understanding of the hare's place in the scheme of things.

The Dee valley was fading fast before the advance of new snows spilling down from the high Cairngorms. All over Morrone, there would be small snow burrowing, small flattenings of moorland grasses. The mountain hares were about to be still again as winter prepared for one more dance down the glen.

Two days later, I was back in the marsh-fringing birches of the Spey, and feeling again how they bridge that landscape chasm between river deep and mountain high. In a matter of fifty feet they have emerged from being creatures of the wetland edge, rarely dryshod, to creatures of the open hill where their presence only dwindles as they begin to rub shoulders with the pine forests. Autumn apart, when the birches blaze briefly through the Cairngorms' one great festival of colour, these winter-into-spring days show the woods at their most charismatic. Birchwoods this far north are silent, pent-up places through this long hybrid season. It is as though the land has drawn its deepest breath and held it, waiting to breathe life into spring, but only when it is convinced spring is ready. Out on the marshes, and on the low fields further up Strathspey, the land breathes more easily, lapwings and oystercatchers make a pied fairground of the place and the first fretful curlews dare a snatched song. Not here, though, not yet.

I climbed through a sun-blessed, wind-spared hour to where the birches wear the texture and lichened rasp of thoughtfully mouldering drystane dyking, the arthritic twist of age which recalled a kinship with the Morrone veterans. I walked myself to a purposeful standstill, watched the fleeting fire on a bullfinch flock, saw it dowse as the finches whistled on. The silence deepened. The sun reddened.

Something stirred beyond the edge of the wood, and, because it encountered only my stillness among the birch trunks, advanced unsuspecting. It was a roebuck in velvet, catching the sun as he leaped a roadside fence, pausing while doe and calf followed suit. They dropped into the gully which fringes the wood, a brief obstacle which gave me time to gain ten yards and a wider tree to attach my stillness to, so that when the buck re-emerged we were at fifty yards and the deer still suspected nothing. Buck and calf converged on the same fragment of woodland floor at the same instant where some succulent tit-bits were briefly disputed. The dispute was undemocratically resolved in the tradition of pecking orders the wild world over – the buck dealt the calf a swift antlered blow in the ribs and the youngster involuntarily backed off.

The doe's head was suddenly high and anxious, staring northwards at some intrusion beyond my field of vision. The buck caught her drift, led a trotting southward retreat, then paused to look back in that endearing roe deer fashion, staring north down his spine while facing south. At a gruff command, the three took the fence at a bound and were gone from the wood and its sunny peace. Moments later, the man and the gun and the black labrador stepped through the gully, crossed the fence, following.

I sat on, imbibing the quiet and the calm, setting this wood's ambience in my mind alongside the heights of Morrone, alongside all the Cairngorms' variations on their birchwood theme. There is rock-climbing Craigellachie above Aviemore, where I tramped half a day in the snow two weeks previously and saw and heard no living creature in four hours until a single chaffinch piped up a monotone to greet my last quarter of a mile (I piped back at him in duotone, and before long he was duotone piping too, a small and amiable exchange which lifted my shrunken spirit); the flat fields of northern Strathspey where the trees flourish straight and slim and shape far prospects to the Lairig Ghru; the autumnal density of Inshriach where the Feshie dips down towards the Spey and where the trees grow tallest, sheltered and rooted in the river itself, and burn their autumn fires longest; the Tomintoul road to the north of the mountains where they wither and warp down the flanks of the hill gorge in deepest March silence, where the wren shreds that silence, havering on and on for ten unbroken minutes at a time.

The birchwoods contribute so much to the Cairngorms landscape, stamping the land with its glacial identity. They were the first trees to stand up and be counted after the Ice, the first to put colour – all-year silver, winter purple, late spring and summer green, autumn flame – back into the palette of the desert which was the land's Ice Age inheritance.

The woodland where I now sat above the Insh Marshes is owned by the Royal Society for the Protection of Birds. I let the silences of my surroundings reimpose themselves, listened intensely to pick out the tiny details of an understorey of sounds – a small burn far off, a restlessness among the whoopers further still, out on the marsh, and nothing, absolutely nothing, else. Then, like an ice-snared burn which leaps forward as the thaw wins through, the silence conceded to the sudden unheralded song of a mistle thrush. The music of it rang in rich, measured phrases and percussive punctuations, welled and flowed until the birchwood brimmed with it, one bird in all that cloistered quiet, yet no Beethoven could have scored a more telling sound. It seemed to stir the wood. A robin threw a song up from the edge of the marsh; five homing rooks rasped down at the treetop thrush spilling black oaths, but the song barely faltered. A blue tit belled softly. The thrush poured mellifluously on and on (I envisaged its song gather and rise and hang like a cloud over the wood's immobility) until at last it paused, and in the immediate aftermath I heard what the song had denied me – the response of a second thrush far across the woods. It was the first short sigh of spring breath in the birchwood.

The RSPB's birchwood is a landscape in good heart. Good birchwoods are good for birds, it is true, but they are also good for birch trees. Managing a birchwood so that it serves the cause of both birds and birches takes time and money and care, creates jobs and makes for beautiful landscapes. I revere – it is not too strong a word – my surroundings. It is not just a beautiful place to be in, it is a beautiful place just to be a birchwood. Look again at the autumn majesty of Inshriach. Look again at what a simple fence has achieved on Morrone, while all around that hillside beyond the fence is a decaying birchwood slum. You look, and you curse the pervasive indifference of the deer forest because its token cull sustains too many red deer and kills too many landscapes.

Then, as if to mitigate the curse, I caught the furtive roe family retracing their steps through the last of the light, stepping deft and dark up the hill into the evening shadow of the pines.

4

.

The Shadow of the Pines

WAXWINGS HUNG from sodden, tight-budded branches like fat grey pears. The wet snow of spring in the lee of the Cairngorms dulled the sheen of them, dulled their watchfulness, so that walking softly I passed eight feet from the nearest of them without disturbing the flock. The snow's soft hiss – it was a sleety hybrid snow creature which stalked the Gleann Einich pines of Rothiemurchus – muted their soft speech.

I walked on a dozen yards to the shelter of thicker pines, stepped into their tangy embrace to pause and look back through the glasses. It was an old birch they had taken to, as far as I could see for no other purpose than to rest and drink from a nearby puddle still rimmed with the ice of the night before. Their conversation carried clear across the forest stillness, an intimate thing of murmured trillings, so soft that I found the brush of the snow-sleet down the pines an irksome barrier to a clear appreciation of the sound.

There is a glitzy fresh-from-the-salon air about waxwings – blow-dried crest, tapered black eye-shadow, a touch of discreet cheek blusher, *haute couture* of dun-grey, black and white and yellow, and the daring scarlet accessories of those sealing wax wingtips which give the bird its name. An Arctic-bound flock of sixty adds nomadic distinction to the glen. They also add sitting-duck variety to the food supply of the natives.

I was quietly folding the moment into my personal anthology of the pinewoods when the sparrowhawk cut her slaty swathe through the white drizzle, twisting between my left knee and the nearest big pine six feet away. She was close enough for the low rasp of air about her wings to cut fleetingly through those other small sounds of sleet-and-bird-murmur. The waxwings scattered, but it was a cumbersome, chaotic scatter, and the slowest had barely cleared the rim of the puddle when it seemed to burst. There was no protest and no contest. The hawk rose, slow now and talon-burdened, faded into the gloom to feed. A litter of grey and tan feathers lodged in the clasp of a juniper tombstone is a fitting and typical pinewood epitaph.

Epitaphs like this the pinewoods can live with. The threads of life and death woven by sparrowhawks and their prey are no more than stitchings in the tapestry of the woods. It is the tapestry itself – now a tattered rag, a frail fragment of the great Caledonian pine forest which once clothed the land with a sprawled majesty – which frays perilously towards extinction. It is true indeed that you cannot contemplate the future of the pinewoods without also contemplating the words 'remnant' or 'relict', for these wondrous woody cloisters have been slaughtered with all the inexcusable thoroughness of a Cumberland among Jacobites.

As yet, you cannot venture far into the Cairngorms without the shadow of the pinewoods falling across your progress. For many people the woods are nothing more than a long trackside dirge. For others they are an end in themselves to which the proximity of the mountains is an irrelevance. For most, in my experience, they are a delight, proclaiming the mountains beyond by their symbolic silhouettes, trees in their true landscape setting. Of all these theories, I deny the first, sympathise with the second, and subscribe unreservedly to the third.

I love the pinewoods. I have often been hijacked by the persuasiveness of their embrace so that I have covered half a dozen green miles instead of twenty mountain miles, and still emerged from the day with my wilderness thirst slaked. To keep the woods' company is to dwell among friends, to be immersed in pools of wilderness, for there are no wilder miles in the land than these. There is no more tenacious clasp on the landscape of the past – the trees reach back in a mere thirty generations to the Ice Age, a startling echo.

But the mountains are no irrelevance. For now, at least, they encircle the pinewoods (once it was the other way round). The pinewoods in turn dignify the mountains, hap their lower slopes warmly against winter's worst excesses, harbour and hold and shield the wildlife, from orchids and ants to ospreys and eagles.

You quickly learn to walk more slowly here. The pinewoods have a way of ensnaring your consciousness. On the drabbest day they impress first with the brightness of the trees, and in this of all lights, when there are no suns to diffuse and deceive, you become aware that not all the pines are green, and not all the green ones are the same shade of green. The darkest shades are the bottlest of greens, almost black; the palest almost grey; then you stumble across a startling yellow tree which once prompted science to consider two species of Caledonian pines, but Seton Gordon helped to scotch that notion seventy years ago – it is a trick of soils.

The deeper in you go, the wilder. I have come now to an old familiar tract of Rothiemurchus. Familiar? I think I know it well, but every new familiarity teaches me principally how little I know of it. I know a thread of a path among the waist-high anthills, which skirts the bogs, and crosses the ones which are easier to cross than skirt. I greet particular trees for something in their attitude; for the death-throes twisting of barkless skin; for a landscape they frame or for wildlife memories they rekindle; for nights asleep under their canopies. I know which parts of the wood offer sudden far sightlines to corrie and plateau, but I never catch my first glimpse of the first snows of autumn etching the glacier-gulp of the Lairig Ghru against darkening skies without also catching my breath. So much is familiar, yet so often so much is seen as it has never been seen before.

Other familiarities are regrettable and salutary. I know, for example, the rough bounds of a roe deer family's territory, yet no matter how doggedly I hug the upwind approach, no matter how discreet of foot my approach, our first new encounter is almost invariably the familiarity of that gruff bark and bouncing white rump of roebuck greeting-in-retreat. The roe are of the woods, and I am not. Each time I come back I must re-acclimatise, shed outside influences, come to terms with sentiments, nostalgias, frustrations, and all the other human frailties and inhibitions which thwart anyone who would become a part of nature's wildest heartland. It takes time. And always you walk too quickly at first.

I had reached a prominent knoll which is a place of small pilgrimage for me each time I return to these woods. It seems to me a pivotal place. For all its meagre elevation, it opens an avenue far up the strath of the Spey; it is mercifully a-bristle with handsome young pines and toddler pines growing footsure in the shade of the old arthritics; it contemplates the western foothills of the Cairngorms, of which the most compelling, Carn Eilrig, is a dark pyramid against the great paling backcloth of Braeriach's northern corries, with their jaunty white cockades of snow cloud. The pines swarm and straggle and finally succumb up the low slopes of Carn Eilrig, and in that conjunction of scattered pines, gathering winter deer and snow-torn heather-moor with the corries piled behind, the mountain elements fuse into a mesmerising profile of the high Cairngorms.

Away to the north, beyond the cloud-brewing highway of the Lairig Ghru, the front rank corries of Cairngorm itself whiten down from their headwalls, a day-long seeping stain, a visible march of the snows. Above all that, the rim of the plateau hardens and blurs and obliterates and re-emerges as high Arctic-cradled storms launch the first fusillades of their winter-long campaign.

So my small eyrie in the pinewoods unites at a lingering glance all the component parts of the greater Cairngorms, all those landscapes over which the mountains hold sway. It *is* a pivotal place, around which revolve not only landscapes but also the thoughts they compel. It is a good place to come and be still and make sense of what it is which sets these mountains apart. I put my back to the soft rasp of ancient bark and sat – in the manner of a pilgrim at the feet of his god, it suddenly struck me – amid the talons of that venerable tree's centuries-old clasp on the Cairngorms soil, in the frail and arrogant human hope that something of the tree's insights nurtured and stored for more than two hundred years might rub off. Mike Tomkies has written of how he tries to grow 'as close to the animal state as possible'. It is an attitude of mind to which he refers, and it is here of all my cherished landscapes that I have come closest to an understanding of what it is he has achieved. I sat. I stilled.

I had been there a long hour, in which the wildest wildlife I saw was a coal tit at fifty yards. It grew darker and colder into the afternoon; south-westerlies sneezed and spluttered icily, nothing as clearly definable as a shower, but a relentless and wearying series of small, stinging assaults which can root deep as a pine into the peaty fertility of an unguarded soul. 'As close to the animal state as possible' – fend it off, reassemble your resolve, a swig at the coffee flask imbibes psychological heat, another long, still hour. Slowly, the senses acclimatise. Ears attune to the speech of the pinewoods, eyes penetrate its folds and delineate its subtleties of shape and form and colour, the wind throws scents as well as stings and scoffing taunts.

Far in the north-west, a high shoulder of Meall a' Bhuachaille shrugged off a heavy-winged bird, thrust it into a purposeful head-on joust with the wind, the one dark fragment of substance in all that intimidating piled might of bruising air which gathered above the mountains and spilled over their flanks. I fastened the glasses on to that unmistakable silhouette now echoed by the land as it crossed Stac na h-Iolaire – rock of the eagle – of Strath Nethy. I tried to fashion in my own mind the tilting Cairngorms of that golden eagle eye and how it might feel to fly head-on into a wall of wind three thousand feet high and as thick as the breadth of the Highlands.

The eagle's course threaded the towering corrugations of the corrie walls of Cairngorm, a procession of hurdles to baulk lesser strides – Coire Laogh Mor, Coire na Ciste, Coire Cas, Coire an t-Sneachda, Coire an Lochain, Creag na Leth-Choin. It is a mighty landscape, mightily defiled, the heart of a piste-skiing empire which can only succeed by destroying the landscape which it cannot do without. Yet this was Seton Gordon writing in 1925:

> In Coire Cas below me there was twilight; through the corrie a drift of ptarmigan flew west in a V-shaped cluster. The eagles were now hunting this corrie. Heedless of the fleeing ptarmigan the two great birds played together, stopping with tightly closed wings at an incredible speed or pursuing one another with eager flight . . . The dusk was deepening as I crossed Coire Cas. Here a stag was guarding a score of mild-eyed hinds and the eagles kept me company, for their hunting had seemingly been unsuccessful, and so they scanned the more eagerly each hiding place for game, feathered or furred . . .

There is no hiding place now in Coire Cas. It is in these few autumn-into-winter weeks of the year alone that an eagle would

judge these northern corries the landscape of a safe passage. The
tourist hordes have gone. The skiing hordes have not yet arrived. This
eagle's traverse of its now derelict arena may well have been the year's
first and last. You do not find eagles where there are no tranquillities,
and the tranquillities in Coire Cas are as thin on the ground as hiding
places. Is there a greater insult we can inflict on a landscape than to
diminish its wildness so utterly that an eagle will shun rock walls and
forest where it once nested and roamed at ease?

The eagle seemed to be working harder for its mileage now as it
crossed the jaws of the Lairig Ghru, Don Quixote tilting at milling
winds. The walls of the Lairig suddenly lower the floor by 1,300 feet,
then, while the bird is adjusting its flight techniques to cope with that
unseen turmoil, fling it up again to restore chaotically the status quo,
or at least as quo as the status of the Cairngorms landscape ever
achieves. But eagles are weaned on turmoils like these. Mastering their
wiles is as crucial and as fundamental to living as learning to outwit
ptarmigan and fox and mountain hare or strip a piece of deer or sheep
carrion. It is necessary, so it is done.

I could sense in my stillness the great bird feel the tugging winds of
the Lairig, and, although it was still too far off to discern even through
the glasses any detailed movement of eagle limbs, I sensed the air's
roar about his head, the rocking stabilising tail, the wristy flexibility of
acres of wing curving to precise command, the splaying and com-
pressing of eighteen-inch primaries, clutching and smoothing down
the erratic air of that Arctic storm.

Those same winds bore the snow clouds of Sron na Lairige deep
into that mighty landscape vee. The downdraught upon an eagle's
back of such a burden is an incomprehensible thrust, but the bird cut a
straight, unwavering line through the storm and came on.

The eagle was westering now, so that the great winds hammered
into his flank, but it kept an even keel despite the immense and
disconcerting lop-sided force. The highest pines of Carn Eilrig fired a
raven on a steep climbing missile arc into the eagle's path. The eagle
flew unswervingly, showed no interest in the intrusion or even
recognition of it until the last unavoidable moment, when a long,
languorous wing administered a decisive swat which so unsettled the
raven that it fell from the combat before it had begun. I have watched

many such encounters where the two birds flickered across the sky, presenting talons, posturing, and relishing (it often seemed) the aerobatics of ritualised conflict, which if it ever became a subject for serious aggression could only have one outcome. I have never before seen one so peremptorily terminated at a single stroke, nor the parting shot administered by a wing.

The raven, in fumbling retreat, could muster nothing more by way of response than a throaty croak. If there was a response to the encounter in the eagle's mind, it was perhaps to steer well to the south of Carn Eilrig and to cross Gleann Einich far to the south of the last pines and their small bird irritants. The last I saw of the eagle, it was beating high over Sgoran Dubh, south-westering again, with the Spey spread beneath, every last mile of it, I fancy, in that late and suddenly brightening afternoon, from source to sea.

The eagle's flight across my sky had been a classic confrontation of the Cairngorms, the stupendous rendered commonplace. These are simply the dimensions of life here, the scale of what it takes to inhabit such a landscape. The wind on the high plateau can kill, not eagle or ptarmigan or snow bunting, which are its mountain kin, but people.

It kills because it deceives. From my wind-blunting pinewood niche the wind on the plateau effects not murder but pageantry. The snow cloud, where it pours down the hillside like a miles-wide waterfall, conveys only its beauty so deep into the pinewoods. In the enchantment of distance, there is no fathoming the lethal qualities it has amassed on its Arctic journeys which now wash the plateau three thousand feet higher than this small knoll.

It is only when you have tested yourself in that wind and felt your throat rasp at its icy dryness, felt your sense of balance falter in the face of its incessant power and overwhelming gusts, felt your resolve wither at its mind-numbing cold grey walls . . . only then that the eagle's matter-of-fact mastery of such airs falls into perspective.

The flight recalled other eagle hours, particularly a long dour day in Lochaber when the birds turned the tables on me. I wrote about it at the time, and, as is so often the case with my eagle-watching, the shade of Mike Tomkies's friendship and influence was at hand. The following is an extract from an account I wrote in the *Edinburgh Evening News*:

At the top of her climb, the bigger, blacker female hung all but motionless for the instant before she landed. Immense dark curves of silhouette wings recalled the words of eagle champion Mike Tomkies. 'Nature's dark angel of death', he called her, and for the first time I saw it his way and shuddered at the power of the metaphor.

The male flew first, a smaller angel, but only by eagle standards, driving east on unbeaten wings. She watched, stepped off, followed, and in her spread-eagled majesty showed a ragged vee wedge of white space deep into one wing.

I followed at my own wingless tread, more because that was the way of my wanderings anyway than in any gesture of pursuit. In my following, the skies piled and lowered and bruised and gathered, and, in the way such times and places do, turned my thoughts deeper in on myself and my golden eagle store. These are sacred moments when something of the wild soul of the hills is within reach, when its wildest heartbeat is a tangible, audible rhythm, when its wildest visions are within sight.

'I go to the Hill to learn its secrets,' Mike Tomkies said. The mighty mass of mountains and all its life from blatant eagles to furtive lichened morsels offered the sesame, offered the hand of its brotherhood for as long as the mood and the whim of the Hill spirits persisted. Deep and dark myself, I took it, and walked among them.

The eagles wrecked it all. I surprised them, grounded, beyond a rise in the glen floor. They rose, heavy bird-burdens for the first slow yards, then split and soared, eagle-powered, to a pair of rocks, two hundred yards apart. Now I was the object of their attentions, a sudden knowledge which brought odd discomfort, the watcher watched.

I scoured the hillside for carrion, prey, clues, straws to clutch at which might explain the grounded birds, found none, climbed down again to wait and watch, aware as I went of my crude efforts to recreate the deepness of the spell that it might embrace the eagles where they sat, but it was gone, and it was not mine to recreate . . .

My Cairngorms golden eagle had crossed my horizon from one corner to the other in perhaps five minutes. I had followed its every

9 Winter sunset over the northern Cairngorms

10   The wild wetlands of the Insh Marshes

11   Nesting coot on the Insh Marshes

12   A flypast of whooper swans over the Insh Marshes

13   Male whooper swan flexes its wings on a marsh lochan

14   Common sandpiper on a lochside tree

15   Wrens climb mountains too!

movement with no greater effort on my part than the slow craning of neck and shoulder muscles as the glasses fastened on to the flight, but in a frenzy of concentration which obliterated every other sight and sound of the pinewoods, even the very consciousness of the surroundings where I sat.

As I relaxed and began to turn over the eagle flight in my mind, these flooded back into the focus of acknowledgment with an almost physical intensity, like the return of blood to frost-bitten feet. They were as blatant as the sound of the river and the bark of roe deer, as subtle as the marauding of crossbills and the mouse-voiced rain of a flock of tits where they rose and fell a hundred yards away, in and out of the vast embrace of an old pinewood giant, Lilliputians with their Gulliver.

Old lessons from other stillnesses in this and other landscapes began to fall into their instinctive place, so that I slid down from that long sitting stillness rather than standing up, and rolled on to my stomach. As my eyes inched above the tallest heather, I met the perplexed gaze of an old red deer hind, newly alerted by some flaw in even that small manoeuvre. Beyond her, two more hinds and two calves grazed on, oblivious. The old one leaned her ears at me, tried to work the wind, but it was not in her favour for the moment, and there was nothing to sustain her wariness. She too bent her head to browse fitfully. In twenty-five minutes the deer had crossed the clearing and stepped leisurely from my sight, which is a reasonable compliment to anyone's stillness. It is not difficult to see red deer in Rothiemurchus, especially in winter, but you must still earn the privilege of close-quartered scrutiny. To watch them walk away unalarmed and at their own pace is no meagre reward.

The spreading stain of light in the south-west which had haloed the last sight of the eagle now dragged the massed clouds of the summits clear of the sun so that a deep yellow fire rushed down Gleann Einich like a tidal bore, fingered into every woody nook of the pines, and, having run its course, lay there, a brimful tidal pool, for as long as the sun commanded the day's last long view of the pinewoods. There was no shred of warmth in it, but I basked in its benevolence and the tricks of light and shadow it worked on the woods' far depths.

Other lights had been shed. It is never a futile exercise trying to penetrate the impenetrable minds of the wildest of wildlife, because it compels thoughtful observation which can only deepen understanding. There will always be much which cannot be understood, but if you trek the same landscape often enough, and ask yourself the same old 'why?' often enough, you will gain access of a kind. I had moved a small step nearer to the animal state in the shadow of the pines.

5

The Tree of the Beginning

THE PROMISE OF MORNING sun tumbled me early from my tent and I beat the sunrise to that part of the pinewoods which opens a wide window on the Lairig Ghru and much of Cairngorm and Braeriach besides. So I followed accustomed practice and put a sound old pine (fifty feet high and fifty feet across the crown and God knows how old) at my back, the better to watch the acute sun dirking down into the mists of the Lairig, unwrapping Braeriach corrie by corrie.

So often the Cairngorms wear shrouds of cloud which ape the contours of the mountains, layering the plateau with a second storey, as though the whole range had been bloated by vast snows thousands of feet deep. In different seasons and different winds and different temperatures, the clouds play different havocs with the Lairig. Today, they simply bridged it, and a trick of the sun lit it from within so that it became a bright tunnel which seemed to burrow into the shining heart of the mountain. Whenever my route lies through these pinewoods, I pause by the tree which signposts this sight. It is a tree in which I have invested a certain symbolic significance – Craobh Toisich, the Tree of the Beginning – because so much has begun for me here over so many years. It has its brother-of-the-pines, well rooted in Gaelic lore, deep in Gleann Einich – Craobh Tillidh, the Tree of the Return – but that is a story for the end of this book. For now, I have paused again by the Tree of the Beginning, the pinewoods' first milestone, to add the sorcery of this early morning winter sunlight to my Cairngorms store in the manner of red squirrels laying in supplies for the lean months ahead.

An eagle was high over Carn Eilrig, so high that I only chanced on the bird with a long, slow and speculative sweep of the glasses, and having watched and lowered them again the eagle quite eluded the naked eye. No amount of scouring the sky could pinpoint it again, and I wondered if it had simply soared into – perhaps clear through – the cloud massif. I was still speculating at life above the clouds on such a morning when I was wrenched back to lowly earthbound reality. The tree at my back had begun to spit. Trees do this in pinewoods, at least the older ones do. There are three possible explanations. Either – and most commonly – it has been raining for an hour beyond the tree's canopy and the rain has now finally forced a resolute way through; or you have been invaded by a flock of crossbills and these are gaudily vandalising the pine cones overhead; or the tree is dizzily hosting a treecreeper.

I followed the sound and the source of a steadily dripping waterfall of bark and found the treecreeper on the upside-down side of a stout bough, stabbing at that fat bark with his puny lance. There is no such manoeuvre in the treecreeper repertoire as a straight line. All life is a corkscrew. This bird had arrived at this tree by way of a dropping, curving flight from the extremities of its nearest neighbour, and begun from a few inches above the roots to spiral up the trunk, delving deep into its massive contours. Bark on a pine this old can be four inches thick and flaky, a mazy paradise for a questing treecreeper.

The bird is a tidily proportioned assembly of slender curves, four-and-a-half inches from stem to stern, off-white beneath, pine-bark grey-brown above, streaked and flecked in white and tawny, the colouring and the curving gathered perfectly about the dark eye by a white curving eye-stripe and the slim rapier down-curve of the bill. A short double-pointed tail tapers palely, a further distinction to the treecreeper's handsome flight profile. All that sleekness is undone, however, by the undercarriage – almost non-existent legs, police-constable feet and a splay of claws which would be outsize on a bird twice as big. But it is with these formidable tools that the treecreeper creeps. Progress up a trunk or out on a limb is a tiny two-footed bouncing gait whether upside-up or upside-down. The claws clasp and the stiffened tail is driven hard into the bark like a wedge. That is part of the treecreeper's secret, but it does not explain either how the bird bounces upside-down without falling off (the wings play no discernible part in the treecreeper's corkscrewing), or why the bird is unable to bounce vertically down a trunk like its Sassunach cousin the nuthatch.

The fascination for me of such an unglamorous pinewood bird as the treecreeper is that it is so totally a bird of the tree. It flies only to reach the next one, and its whole world is that shady, woody realm between bark and trunk. There it eats, roosts and nests wherever a piece of vintage bark can be prised loose enough to be a nursery for anything up to ten chicks, and stays secure enough to blind the attentions of a hunting owl or thwart the sting of spring storms.

Now the treecreeper of the Tree of the Beginning crash-landed on the bark at the junction of trunk and limb in the kind of head-down-upside-down attitude which must confound thoughtful navigation. He spiralled upwards – and found that the spiral wrapped not the trunk but the limb – a bouncing yard, a bark-stabbing pause, two bouncing yards, a plucked fly, and so on until he had exhausted that limb's possibilities, fluttered out to the extremity of the next one, and began corkscrewing back in towards the trunk. The entire tree was cross-examined in this fashion, until the bird fell from one particularly high and frail branch, dived down to the bottom of the next trunk and began again. I would guess at a treecreeping-to-flying ratio of about two hundred to one.

The extremes of nature have a way of tripping over each other in the Cairngorms. Here I was jerked from eagle to treecreeper. One is the bird which stravaigs all these skies and throws its feared shadow over every tussock from the moors to the summits; the other is a bird which shuns skies and scarcely throws a shadow at all in its flimsy shaded flights of a handful of descending yards. Yet both are happy to nest in pine trees. One builds so hugely that it changes the shape of trees, the other so furtively, and using the *inside* of the tree, that most of us could stand five paces away and see nothing.

Or you stand in awe of some high summer sun-and-cloud show hurtling rainbows in a juggler's arc across a dozen huge corries, then suddenly look down to find the discreet and elusive glories of twinflower or creeping ladies' tresses at your feet, or to find a marching army of ants has adjusted to the new contours you have just inflicted on its path and is crossing your left boot five or six abreast.

These ants are a phenomenon of the pinewoods. They build vast domed cities from dead pine needles, layer upon decomposing layer, ferrying them distances of yards, scurrying through every season but deepest winter. Something of the timelessness of the mountains pervades the ritual of their work, something almost sinister attends the unstoppable seething yet functional pinewood Tokyos they inhabit. I love the inferences of Norman MacCaig's poem, 'Another Incident':

> In the pass between
> the four great bens of the Cairngorms
> an ant
> climbed down a pinetree.
>
> One followed it, and another, till
> an unceasing narrow procession
> filed through the tangled grass.
> In their path my tent opened
> its huge cave.
>
> I began by killing them.
>
> When one stumbled across
> the corpse of a brother
> he raised him high in his jaws
> and bustled off with him.
>
> If, a million generations from now,
> a descendant of mine returns here,
> he'll find a procession of ants
> filing on the plain
> where the four great bens of the Cairngorms
> once used to be.

There are times, when the anthills reach four feet in height and half a dozen in width (the dimensions of years of pine needles), that you begin to suspect the ants of Cairngorms-sized ambition, and more than once I've fancied I've seen the shape of Meall a Bhuachaille or

Gael Charn or Bynack Mor echoed in an anthill. There is a thread of life, and a thread of imagination, inextricably woven, which stitches ant to eagle.

The treecreeper, which had tripped over my eagle-wedded thoughts, was moving around the winter woods in a flock of tits. Suddenly a swagger of coal tits, bright blue tits, and other small jingling flotsam of the woods swarmed into the Tree of the Beginning. From their jaunty, jiving midst, there emerged a flicker of pied bravado, a piercing three syllable greeting, and one of the ultimate and exclusive delights of the pinewoods had hurtled down to an upended landing on a branch five feet away. I have never had a crested tit in the camera viewfinder before and been too close to focus the lens. There he stayed for ten inexorable seconds, which is a mighty stillness for a cresty, while I peered *over* the lens and the sun glittered in his ebony eye. Crested tits are drab, forgettable little birds from the neck down, but from the neck up they wear startling distinctions. There is first a black bib, then a black collar, then a white collar, then a black Picasso tattoo on each white cheek, then the pied and pointed crest vividly patterned like a crossword grid gone terribly wrong.

The birds' second distinction is that although they are not rare in the pinewoods of the Cairngorms they occur almost nowhere else in Britain in any numbers (and show a marked preference for Speyside even within their specialised landscape bias). They are so thirled to their pinewood domain that instincts hold the young birds within a mile of their nest for life. Only in extraordinarily mild winters is that rule flaunted, when an abnormally high winter survival will persuade a few to fly in the face of their sedentary instincts to new horizons, or at least new pinewoods.

The trailblazing pair which turned up on Deeside in 1950, for example, invited the speculation among local naturalists that they had crossed in the time-honoured fashion of all travellers from Spey to Dee, by the Lairig Ghru. Imagine the forces at work in those tiny bird brains which propelled such a daring defiance of instinct! Imagine the restless flights around the nursery woods in search of territory, the slow abandonment of instinct as one fragment of forest after another revealed the pied patchwork crests, echoed to soft warnings. Imagine the hesitant climb through the highest pinewood stragglers, then, on wings with which others of their tribe might never dare a flight of more than two or three hundred yards at a stretch, the commitment to flight across fifteen of the most hostile and unequivocally treeless miles in the Highlands.

What might they have made of that darkening defile under Lurcher's Crag, or the boulderfield which sets such a foot-fankling obstacle for walkers in the throat of the pass, or the new chill air as they crossed the Pools of Dee at three thousand feet. Oh to have been taking my well-earned ease by the Pools on that day and watched through barely believing eyes the bird mites advance over the last of the boulders, as irrelevant in that landscape scheme of things as thistledown, then tremble down to the poolside, two crested tits in search of the promised land!

As the birds flew south, did they baulk at the gape of An Garbh Coire, which at first glance has all the hallmarks and dimensions of a second Lairig Ghru carving away west? Was that the way to the promised land? Or did they acknowledge, by instinct or by navigational craft, that the corrie's burn was an upstream water, and that the trees would surely lie downstream, for all upstreams hereabouts led to the tree deserts of corrie headwalls and snow-scrolled plateaux?

When they reached the first deer-plagued pines of Glen Dee, would they sense a journey's end, a new beginning, one small step for the titmouse tribe? Or would nothing register beyond the fulfilment of nature's command – it was done because it was required to be done?

I have launched many journeys from the Tree of the Beginning. A few of them were simply journeys of the mind.

Five days before Christmas and three nights before the full moon, I walked deep into the pinewood night. There was not the white blaze of light I had hoped for, no miles-wide mountain silhouette, but the moon flooded the high cloud cover so that the sky, instead of the stark black of a cloudless winter night, was a fast-moving tumult of pale shadows propelled by high winds which made almost no impression at all in the pinewoods. The paleness of the sky had two benefits. One was that it served to silhouette anything which flew – and almost at once a tawny owl slipped silently out from high on a pine, looking small and compact and blunt and so much more a fragment of his world in nocturnal guise than the bird you are inclined to stumble across in roosting daylight. The second benefit to night eyes was that every tree above the lowest darkest common denominator of the pinewoods stood clearly defined, so that the birches, which in winter daylight melt non-committally into the overwhelming density of the pines, now advanced to be recognised in every twiggy detail. The pines, by comparison, are hard two-dimensional shapes, quite twig-less. I was surprised at how much birch I was seeing, for it is only in autumn that the briefly blazing birches reveal their true numbers in pinewood daylight, and by Christmas autumn is a long season away.

The deceptions of the pinewood night are at ground level, where every juniper bush becomes everything else in the flights of your imagination . . . deer, watching figures, foxes (once, I was so con-vinced I was downwind of a big dog fox I even contrived a fox smell from what turned into one more juniper bush).

I came again to my Tree of the Beginning, and put the unfamiliar brushstrokes of night to that old familiar canvas – the suddenly open forest, the widespread mountains, the Lairig Ghru, indistinguishable in this light from all other Cairngorms shades. The corries, too, those great thumbprints of Cairngorm and Braeriach, were undefined, and only the pallor of the sky delineated the mountain shapes. The moon punched holes in the thick cloud, and, through these, stars would flicker and fade like erratic lighthouses. It seemed a huge sky of bloated clouds, some shadowed by others crossing them at a greater height and at a greater windspeed. The clouds seemed low, but the mountains were well clear, and there was probably no cloud lower than 4,500 feet. Even the mountains looked low and squat, as though in the night they had withdrawn a little from the world.

You must move through the night woods by a different set of rules. I took my accustomed seat by the pine, trying to tune in to the landscape of the dark. I listened first to the wind, because it is the first song of the night woods. If there is wind, it dominates sound utterly. If there is none, its absence dominates.

As I listened, the intensity of the listening deepened. I began to disassemble the wind. The most obvious wind was in the branches of my tree. I set that as the pitch to offset all the other winds, a kind of middle C of the woods. A deeper wind was at work in the body of the trees I had just left, playing on the mass of flat crowns. A smaller, higher wind danced through the litter of the pinewood floor, making small songs of the carpet of needles, strong enough to tremble a fallen cone, but not strong enough to move it. The smallest wind, felt rather than heard, was nibbling round the trunk by my head, and straight into my right ear. I tried, in the sudden awareness of the minute nature of that last wind, to catch some strain of the great mountain wind ravaging the far tops, but it was bearing its own voice away from me, and no shred of its shouting banshee reached me.

But I had made a chord of the wind with four clear pitches. The distractions of daylight would never permit such a thing.

I walked another hour into the forest. Nothing moved other than the wind-stirrings of the trees, the race of the clouds. I felt curiously lonely, which is not a problem I often encounter when I am alone of my own volition in the wilds. I found the problem rooted in that idea that nothing else moved in the forest. What rubbish! Nothing moving? In a forest like this? The problem, of course, was that I couldn't see or hear anything move, and, apart from my phantom fox scent, couldn't smell anything either. There was nothing for me to fear, but I was quite unable to shed a disconcerting uncertainty, fuelled I think by the nature of the forest half-light which grew more eerie as I watched it.

The wildlife of the daylight forest would question my presence and defer to it, the deer running before me, the fox circling far upwind to catch my scent, the red squirrel retreating at a high vertical gallop, the capercaillie clattering violently through the branches, the wildcat lying low. Some of those responses can be mitigated by the stalker's stealth, the naturalist's brain, the watcher's still eye. The wildlife of the night forest, though, is the superior race, moving, resting, hunting without uncertainty. Would it sense not only my presence but also the uncertainty of my presence? I turned back, humbled and troubled by the wild woods, sadly and darkly aware of the distance which the everyday life of any mere mortal inflicts on such an elusive ambition as a closeness to the animal state.

It turned into a long, sleepless, wild, cold night in the tent. The same ground on which I had slept for a week was suddenly an inhospitable shelf of roots and rocks. The wind grew and grew, and at its zenith its angriest gusts hurtled across the pine tops like one of those earliest stereophonic records of a train going through a tunnel. By five I had lit the stove in the tent to warm the air, and as soon as I could tolerate uncovered hand and face I brewed tea and settled to drink till dawn. I lit a candle, and as the stove steamed and the tea thawed out the mind I scribbled the night down in pencilled telegramese. I quote the last couple of lines as I wrote them, yawning hugely, somewhere about six in the morning in a shuddering tent besieged by falling pine cones, deafened by wind and now rain, four days before Christmas and two nights before a full moon: 'All this on day of HRC [Highland Regional Council] review advocating skiing expansion into Lurcher's. How many of them have sat in a pinewood at night and made a chord of the wind?'

The morning after all that passed in a sleety haze. I dozed, woke to a new wind-and-rain assault on the tent, dozed and woke to brew more tea, dozed and finally woke to an absence of sound. It was noon when I thrust weary eyes out at the wood. It glittered in a grey sort of way. Every branch, twig, cone and needle was rimmed or rounded off by clinging raindrops. There was almost no light, although the day would grow no brighter. If your morale can withstand solitude in those barely breathing late December days of semi-permanent Highland darkness, you are well equipped to handle most of what life can throw at you, for their dourness seeps into your bones and infiltrates your spirit like a dulling drug. The song of such days is a threnody, but even threnodies have their rhythms, and you survive by learning to move to that rhythm, by tuning in to the landscape's slowest heartbeat, by slowing and stilling in time to its longest pauses. I shrugged off the night, and wandered back more or less aimlessly, following easily my own spoor of the night before, for nothing and no one had stepped that way since.

As I walked, I made no effort to be cheerful. I have no rituals of raising my own spirits when I am alone in the wilds, but rather respond to the prevailing mood of the land. If the land is down-hearted, I sympathise with it, and in that way stay close to it. Walking in company is different, for then tribal loyalties hold sway and you move to a different rhythm. If your only conversation is with the landscape, however, you cannot fill a subdued day with shouts and whistles and songs and laughter. So I made my way softly and subdued, with many short stillnesses to catch the pulse of the land. I started to study individual trees as they approached and slipped past, following shape and form and colour with an eye now well attuned to such pinewood subtleties, until it came to rest on a Goliath of a tree whose dominating position had somehow escaped me previously, although I had passed within a dozen yards of it countless times in twenty years.

It is well screened from the track by a small stockade of birches and junipers and lesser pines, and these conspire to shield something of its immensity. But today I stepped directly into a clearing which lent the tree the arena it demanded for its showpiece qualities, for its classical Scots pine form, flat-crowned, rounded silhouette, a mighty spread of akimbo limbs, and a double trunk as vast and resolute as its proportions demanded. A complete circuit of the tree was a heady progress. It was perhaps seventy feet high, perhaps twenty feet round the base of that double trunk. One root was at least two feet thick, its bark four inches deep in places and contoured like a relief map of an incomprehensible landscape.

A withering of grey moss coated much of the bark as if in its great age the tree had grown a fine flowing beard, but it seemed to suggest too the tumbling vegetation and craggy contours of an eagle eyrie cliff I know. If the eagle is King of Birds, then this was certainly a golden eagle among pines.

The vee of the tree's great fork, from which the two trunks soared to their separate heights, had also accumulated a small landscape of its own. Here, over centuries, all manner of wind-blown forest leftovers had embedded, amassing their own haphazard contours. Over these, golden waterfalls of spent pine needles cascaded and lodged. In the tiny heart of that miniature tree-born landscape, a birch had rooted and grown, slender and straight, to a sapling of three feet. So the venerable Scots pine, which must have spawned so many generations of its own tribe, but which was now too old to offer much in the way of regeneration, has taken on the role of foster mother to a birch. Such is the company you can keep when you walk alone in the pinewoods of the Cairngorms.

Such is the hold the finest of pinewood individualists command that you catch yourself nodding to a few favoured trees as you pass. It is a short step from the kind of familiarity which prompts such a ritualised gesture to the degree of intimacy with which the Gaelic language, a knowing tongue, once named every landscape feature. A random search through any roll-call of the place names of the Cairngorms would unearth such as Cnap Coire na Spreidhe – Knoll of the Hollow of the Livestock; Gleann Tromaidh – Valley of the Dwarf Elder Tree; Sron Bhuirich – Promontory of Roarings . . . and Craobh Tillidh – the Tree of the Return. So I first nodded to my pine tree which fingerposts the serried might of the Cairngorms, and, in the manner of much which has gone before over many centuries, I have christened it. Craobh Toisich, Tree of the Beginning – although it is unlikely ever to be absorbed into those same lists of place names, it has its honoured place in the roll-call of my mind whenever I am preoccupied by the Cairngorms and their pinewoods.

The rain began again, dragging the sky down with it. I was back at the tent by three, by which time it was quite dark; it would be eighteen hours before anything like daylight broke over the pinewoods again. By five I had dismantled my tent, stowed my sodden gear, driven a dozen Speyside miles, and was enjoying a substantial dram before Cameron McNeish's fire. For a day or two at least, the pinewoods had got the better of me.

6

In the Court of the Monarch

THREE TRUTHS CONFRONT the deer-watcher in the Caledonian pinewoods of the Cairngorms. The first is that these woods are beleaguered by deer. There are far too many animals and far too few naturally regenerating pines. In the eastern Cairngorms in particular, the pinewoods are dying on their feet in glen after glen.

The second truth was spoken to me by a seasoned forester friend. He said simply, 'a forest is not a forest without deer.' He was right. The red deer of Scotland are foresters by instinct and ancestry, for all the evictions which recent centuries have inflicted on them. They are stunted shadows of their old deep forest forebears, poor imitations of their forest-dwelling European kin. In pinewoods such as these they are part of the natural scheme of things, provided their numbers are controlled at levels which permit the young trees to thrive.

There is a third truth, a singularly human response, admittedly, but one to which I cheerfully own up. It is that a handsome beast is at its best in a handsome setting. I have watched gannets fish the turgid waters of the Forth with supertankers for fellow-travellers and blurred petro-chemical this-and-thats for a backcloth in the binoculars. I have also watched them in south Skye where the following glass drags across the profile of Rhum and the blazing west, and I know which I prefer, and for that matter where the bird fares best. You can watch a roe in Leicester or Lothian, but in the pinewoods of the Cairngorms he is a beast of wilderness and lives by its laws, the laws which best befit the wildest of nature's bestiary. The trees and the deer, whether red or roe, are at their best when the one frames the other, because they belong mutually.

There was that day, autumns ago, when I sat in the pines of Gleann Quoich under Beinn a Bhuird with six hours on that crudely lacerated mountain behind me (October ice on its plateau lochans, a thin fur of snow on the ice). I paused for two more hours in the pinewoods' afternoon sunlight, a moving, healing respite. I had been there a long hour when the woods around me exploded with the stamping of many feet, the jarring clash of antlered heads, the grating throb of stag-bellow, the symphonic discord of what for me is one of the finest hours in nature's ritual year, the red deer rut.

I have watched the rut many times in many mountain glens, but never before had I seen it or even contemplated it in a setting of trees. The fundamental difference is that it announces itself while it is still invisible, so that its approaching tensions infect all in its path, which on this occasion included me. I dared not move for fear of what I might miss, yet for the first time I knew fear in the presence of red deer.

The hinds entered the arena of trees first, and at a placid trot which immediately devalued the furore of the overture. I had anticipated a wild-eyed strewn panic, forgetting in the disturbing moments of their advance that it is simply not in the nature of the hinds to be panicked by the stags' outraged jousts and jealousies. Here, as on the open hill, they wandered at will, and the stags followed them. The hinds, fourteen of them, strayed casually to the river, and stopped to drink while the stags' battleground shifted unnervingly behind my back. The knowledge that I now sat between the stags and the hinds did nothing to allay my steadily maturing fears. I was suddenly in some awe of the wildlife all around me, nakedly aware of the fact that they were in their element and I was not.

There was a tremulous clash of antlers behind, the soft thunder of heather-happed hooves, and a young stag burst in on the hinds' arena two yards to my left. There uncoiled then, the same distance to my right, the rawest, most awesome noise I have ever heard this side of a snow avalanche. My head jerked right. The master stag entered, peat-blackened, hoary-muzzled, thick-chested, high-headed, wide-antlered, barrel-necked, and, with the wind working mercifully in my favour, he stank. In that moment I granted Landseer all the credibility I had hitherto always denied him. Here was one Victorian fantasy which had just passed its test of time in the most eyeballingly-convincing fashion. Monarch he was.

He advanced four slow strides towards the young stag now thrusting his attentions on one straying hind. At the sound of the master's first quickening stride, though, the young animal turned abruptly to face his great rival, then with a clear gesture like a shying horse swerved off with a fast sideways movement. He conceded.

By the time the master stag was halfway across the clearing the young beast was in retreat and heading for an alley in the trees, a path which, by a trick of fate or a kindly gesture of some God-of-the-deer, propelled him head-on towards the flank of the stray hind. She, with all options removed, ran before him, so that in his hour of defeat, and quite involuntarily, he had gleaned the first bride of his harem.

The master stag, now braking to negotiate more trees, seemed to contemplate pursuit, but at a bark and a purposeful stride from the matriarchal hind he stopped dead, hurled a second bellowed rebuke at the retreating stag, turned to outflank the movement of the hinds back the way they had come. They went anyway, and, his style cramped by the intrusion of more trees, he had no option but to follow, his honour satisfied, but with only thirteen hinds at his majestic disposal. The whole episode, from first inklings to last gasp, had taken perhaps a minute and a half. In the moments that followed, in the stunned sunny silence through which I sat in a state of privileged shock, I could see, hear, sense nothing. It was the stench of deer on the air which unlocked the trance, the deftly oblivious bark-spitting quest of a hunting treecreeper above my head which banished it.

So that was my vindication of that simple philosophy that 'a forest is not a forest without deer', my vindication of my own preference for a handsome landscape in which to confront a handsome beast. The pinewood *is* the deer's place. It is our place, in the absence of natural deer predators, to ensure that there are not too many deer for the good of the pinewoods, and for that matter that there are never too few pinewoods for their own good. It is not a complex equation, but those vested landowning interests which hold too many deer so that they can be shot for profit keep a stranglehold on the possibility of progress.

Rothiemurchus estate demonstrates eloquently enough that it can be solved, however. The estate's own Visitors' Guide and Footpath Map, thoughtfully provided free in little bird-box-sized containers around the estate, says:

> Control of [deer] numbers by man is essential as most of their natural predators such as wolves now only roam in the wildlife park. This ensures the wellbeing of the population which is maintained in balance with the environment. The population is held at a level which does not cause excessive damage to naturally regenerating pine seedlings by browsing. Deer management is essential for the conservation of both the pine forest and the deer herd . . .

There is a first commandment of Cairngorms land management enshrined in that simple philosophy.

I tested the wind by the mouth of the glen where the pines fan out into a heathery parkland, and put a wide southerly mile on to my preferred route so that I might cross the parkland head-on to the wind, easing up into the thickening crag-clinging trees, contouring round into the highest pinewood corrie of all. That way, I hoped to put red deer and roe across my path, and see something of the best of that balance of deer and pines at work.

I was well into my detour before anything moved, but it was no deer. She had been feeding on a rock where the bloodied remains of blue tit told their own tiny obituary, but she was up at my advance with her searing dash, away with the colour of the moor clinging to her. The smallest hookbeak in the wilds, the smallest falcon wings, the most spellbinding moorland wizardry – merlin wizardry, to which I have never been immune.

She was lost to the moor in seconds, but arced back into sight far out on a pine runt, so far out that I marvelled again at such moor-devouring strides in such a slip of a bird. It is a deceptive daintiness, for she is a thoroughbred falcon and so a lethally efficient killer. In the long dead days when the falcon on your gloved hand was your passport to the upper reaches of society, a sort of mediaeval American Express, she was the ladies' bird, falconry made feminine.

There are few enough falconers now to indulge their bird-slavery games, still fewer who fly a merlin to the lure, because it takes a moor like this to succour a brood of merlins, and moors like this are as thin on the ground as . . . well, merlins. It is a recurring dilemma of the Cairngorms that all its distinctive habitats are dwindling and at risk, and that if you plead for one there is a vested interest which will demand a slice of another by way of compensation, and if you plead for both there is someone to decry you for your conservationist's greed or your élitism. But the place is only what it is because it is the sum of its exquisite parts, and its uniqueness can only survive if it survives intact, so even as you plead for the pinewoods you must also plead for the moor, the corries, the plateau.

The moor has all but lost the right to be a moor, because it is always a potential something else. It is a potential field with a Department grant. It is a potential forest plantation with a Commission grant. It is a potential grouse moor with a hefty financial incentive from rich European shooters who don't have a decent grouse moor the length of their land. Moors should not be confused with grouse moors. There are grouse on them, to be sure, but on the grouse moor the heather is carefully burned, predators are carefully controlled, keepering is practised diligently (and too often, still, illegally). The grouse is all. On the moor, the heather grows the way nature permits, the merlin weaves its wizardry, harriers and owl skulk slowly over the heather, eagles prospect the skies and the grouse take their chances with the rest. The only inducement to leave a moor in peace is the long, slow richness of looking at a moor left in peace. There ought to be a Ministry or a Commission to give a damn about that, but there is not.

The merlin's tide, like the moor's, is on the ebb, and this bird's small imprint on my deer-journeying suggests another reason other than the moor-dwindling. It is that the bird is simply too wee for its own good, and too furtive of flight to capture the imagination of the bird-loving world. It is easy to be moved by eagle or osprey for their blatant spectacle, or a kestrel for its confiding way of hanging over the most tamed of man's landscapes. A buzzard spirals and mews on the wind and your wild soul aches. A merlin strikes down a blue tit in blurring level flight, and you blinked and missed it.

The word 'merlin' carries its first dodo-taint of extinction; it is already scarcer than the golden eagle, and I am always aware that the last time I saw a merlin could prove to be the last time I saw a merlin.

That single scrap of merlin flight was to be all that day granted me, and as the afternoon dwindled and darkened I felt increasingly as though I had become the object of a conspiracy of the wilds. For four more hours, I trekked and contoured the pinewoods until I had drained all but the last dregs of daylight from the afternoon. I saw and heard nothing. Not a deer, not a bird, not a scrap of song or glimpse of far flight, not a scrape of vole or a gleam of squirrel, no snatch of sun to lighten the shadow of the pines grown suddenly burdensome. The wind rose and a thin sleety rain stooped on my path like a peregrine on a teal. In that glowering afternoon I became as unfit for human company as I have ever been. In its last darkening hour, I sat by a small burn high in the pine-filled corrie to brew coffee. I took out a writing pad and pencil while the stove muttered under the pan, for I like to write in intimate response to physical surroundings, being 'there' in Mallory's phrase.

Infinite depths of trees rose ahead, behind, and to the left, fell away to the right. Through these, cloud splinters drifted while an unbroken mass of darker cloud the breadth of the Highlands bore down and down. I fell into the abyss of that afternoon.

I sat there another twilit hour of which I can remember absolutely nothing. I was incapable of thought, my instincts enfeebled by the conspiracy. All that happened was that I simply sat, an unshackled prisoner of the conspirators. I sat until some subconscious internal force, uneasy at what must have felt like the onset of hibernation, began trying to prise me out of that grey hour's ensnaring clasp, loosening bonds, stoking instinct, demanding human response – wariness, assessment, movement. I became for brief moments the focal point of an ancient conflict. Men may have won a physical mastery over the land, but only as a collective, bludgeoning army. Isolate the individual from the tribal strength, put him alone in one wild corner of the most primeval of landscapes, have the unnerving unseen forces of that landscape marshall their own tribal offensives and he is its most vulnerable, ragged-nerved creature.

I stirred to an unease for all my familiarity with that place, my sensibilities strove like a butterfly hell-bent on flight after the strictures of the chrysalis. I noticed first an alien stench, a hot metallic air which I instinctively resented in such a place. It was my own pan on my own stove, long boiled dry and slowly turning brown. In the process of reaching absently to remove it, swearing at the burning heat of the handle, flipping the pan with a boot into the burn where it spat madly then fell silent, I broke what remained of the spell. The writer's page was blank and dampening. I rose, packed, walked. The four miles to the tent drifted past, tree by tree by tree.

I slept late, breakfasted slowly, contemplated a hard fast climb on to the plateau for its icy-airy refreshment, but the thought died, still-born, overwhelmed by the new thought that you go to the plateau only when you seek it out for its own sake, not so that you can disavow the pinewoods. By noon I was back among the high pines, breathless on a boulder, and the nearest rock had just spoken sharply to the nearest juniper, a stiff monosyllabic command.

From behind the rock stepped a roe doe in anxious, hesitant retreat. She walked, rather than bounded, away, pausing often to stare at the juniper and at me. I photographed her twice while she stood for me, then put the glasses on her. She was wintering well, her rich dark brown coat and white rump patch a handsome livery. The grey patch at her throat and the neck ring of brown suggested a seasonally appropriate scarf. She barked again, stamped a foot at my stillness, and this time the juniper spilled her miniature mirror image in reluctant obedience, truculent as a child.

The fawn ambled towards her mother's barely contained impatience, but halfway between the roe and me she caught some fickle trick of the pinewood wind or some inaudible communication of her mother's tension, for she stopped in mid-stride, stared at me over her shoulder and down the length of her back. The gesture permits an animal to scrutinise danger behind when the confines of her surroundings may not always permit turning quickly, and also affords a quicker escape because she is already facing in the direction of safety. But the fawn was merely insatiably curious. Twice more the adult deer barked, each bark producing a response of a couple of reluctant strides from the kid, then another long standing scrutiny of the boulder where I crouched.

It was the impatience of the mother which snapped. She barked again in a noticeably sharper voice and spring-heeled a brief retreat up fifty feet of hillside, where she stopped to assess its effect on the fawn. It was a meticulously judged tactic. She sprang after her mother, and although she could muster little more than half the adult's pace her confident way with that steep and foot-fankling forest floor had a quite mesmerising beauty. When she reached her mother there was a muffled rebuke, and the pair took to the slope again, their hocks and blazing white rumps jostling away almost in a unison of movement. They began to contour away east, which would put the scent of my pursuit on the wind, so I sat on for ten minutes and then began a slow parallel contour a hundred feet below their line of retreat. I found them again in ten more minutes.

I crawled the last dozen yards to a rock, pleased with myself for stalking so close and unobserved to a pair of deer who would still be uneasily wary from our first encounter. In the lee of the rock I unpacked the camera, manoeuvred with my own definition of silence on to my knees, gingered into position to take photographs of two untroubled deer browsing blissfully. I focused instead on an empty clearing, lowered the camera, found the doe in the deepest trees above the clearing and staring down at me, ears cocked, head angled, fawn tucked warily behind her, troubled and unblissful. Her vigilant superiority thus re-established, she simply turned and walked away, her fawn at her heel. As close to the animal state as possible – would it ever be close enough?

I sank down behind the rock, drew long and deep and reflectively on the coffee flask and the sprawled panorama of the Spey and the Monadhliaths beyond, Loch an Eilein with its osprey-haunted ruin, the ragged-pile carpet of Rothiemurchus, 'the wide plain of the firs', snow-ridged Meall a Bhuachaille's Mount Fuji impersonations. There was a light snow on the pinewood air, frail as moths. I turned back to the deer.

The doe had barely moved, browsing testily, stopping to stand and stare again at my renewed interest. My presence or at least my stillness seemed more of a puzzlement now than a blatant threat. Once, she took three strides towards me, angled her head in a profound study of concentration. What was she thinking? *Was* she thinking? I watched her hard through the glasses, and it seemed that this head-on scrutiny was a more thoughtful, less fearful consideration than the over-the-shoulder ready-to-run approach. Whatever her conclusions, she walked no more than a dozen yards, and, having stationed herself conspicuously between me and her now wholly uninterested fawn, began to browse again.

The snow thickened. As she moved comfortably away I followed, keeping well behind, and thirty feet downhill. The fawn ambled along above her on a parallel track, and for a hundred yards of that ancient mountain forest I followed step for step, as hand-in-glove with the land as I have ever walked.

In the screening of the falling snow, I came closer to the roe, and when she stopped and bent to browse again I stopped tree-still and unaccountably expectant. What happened next has something to do with the privilege and the prize which is to be won through paying your dues to the landscape. For every hour I have sat enthralled among trees like these or skulked the deer tracks, or gloried in the corrie walls or basked in the heady eagle-scrolled spaces of the plateau in the various states of the wild seasons' wellbeing, I have watched ten more wither away in forgettable frustration, ill-pleased with my addiction to wildness. There has come, however, among the joyous hours, a thin gleaning of indefinable moments when the very soul of wildness, the very lives of birds and beasts are accessible. I now encountered one such moment, for an awareness had grown, sloth-slow, that I had ceased to be a mere observer. I experienced such a profound fellow-feeling with the place and its winter lives that I swam now in the kind, wild whirlpool of that fellowship. I was bound by its quiet revolutions, explored its unturbulent depths, yet I was conscious as I watched that another sitting by me would not have seen as I saw or learn as I learned, for that is the prize.

I saw first the fawn's ears switch forward, her ambling gait halt abruptly, her head angle sharply, and in that attitude she froze. She was ten feet higher up the hillside than her mother, and for the moment she could see what her mother could not. The doe had seen only the fawn's reaction, sensed from it the presence of a disturbing influence. From my position twenty feet below the doe, I could see the cause for concern – a stoat in ermine trim running easily along the deer track towards the hidden doe. First the stoat saw the fawn, all eyes and ears, ten feet above him, and that stopped him dead. He stood, in the manner of all musteloids, on his hind legs, brandishing his curiosity like a clan tartan, checked by some sixth sense of forboding. The doe came on, head low, nose working, ears flickering warily, anxious for scent and sound. The stoat dropped on all fours, ran on, checked, stood, dropped, hesitated, stood, then in a frenzy of decisiveness hurtled flat out round the corner of a rock to meet the level gaze of the doe three feet away. The doe's feet splayed wide and her head went down, an attitude so like a Disney cliché that I caught myself grinning hugely. The stoat braked and reared in the same movement, an eloquent feat of coordination and reflex, and for perhaps two seconds took stock of the sorcery which had befallen him.

One instant he had ducked down past what he would recognise as a young – and therefore small – roe deer, the next his path was blocked by its mirror image, hideously magnified. His response was to take the rock face – all eight feet of it – in three bounds, a Messner-ish feat of climbing which had the unnerving consequence of landing him by the ankles of the fawn. Here, he performed the nearest thing I have ever seen to a double-take in the wild, a spine-stretching assessment of first the fawn then the doe. He stood taller then, and saw beyond the doe the real enemy which finally snapped his nerve – me.

He plunged into the undergrowth; the doe watched him go, then sensed my presence. There was one more command to the fawn, which responded eagerly now, and they stepped off in tandem into the deepest wood, into the thickening snow.

That left only me. I leaned back against the nearest tree, as magnetised by the empty stage as I had been by the performance. It was then that the previous day's encounter with the abyss reasserted itself, and, by a trick of the psychological forces which anyone going alone into wild landscape must combat constantly, suddenly assumed a predatory aspect I found vaguely disconcerting. But now I was forewarned by the events of the day before, buoyed by the events of today. I shouldered my pack, and prepared to leave.

Precisely at that moment, a fluke of sightlines through the trees showed Braeriach ablaze with new snow and a late afternoon jig of sunlight about that singular mountain's corries and cloud caps, and my spirit was fired too. By throwing a single glance from the stoat on the forest floor to the sun on the plateau, I had begun to recognise something of their kinship within the same landscape. I walked out with my twin anthems of the pinewoods ringing in my ears: 'as close to the animal state as possible . . . '; 'a forest is not a forest without deer . . . '

7

The Forgiveness of Nature

EARLY APRIL, Glen Derry, a midnight walk under a big moon (antidote to a wretched day and a long cross-country drive through walls of rain, roads like rivers), snow down to two thousand feet and the mountain world brighter lit and better defined than many a midwinter noon. Somewhere about one-thirty I clambered into my sleeping bag to doze a couple of hours under the stars, intent on climbing through the dawn to a high breakfast. Somewhere about two-thirty I jerked awake at the sound of bathwater running down the plughole. I assembled what scattered fragments of consciousness I could muster and brought them sluggishly to bear on the sound, which seemed to be coming from high in a pine tree to my right. The bathwater routine suddenly degenerated into something like a recording of a drumming woodpecker fiendishly slowed down and hideously magnified. It crossed my mind then that I was still asleep and dreaming weirdly.

It took some time before I recognised it for what it was – the preposterous pre-dawn vocabulary of a cock capercaillie, precursor of the early morning rituals of the lek.

Within an hour of more bathwatering and deformed woodpecker-ing the vast silhouette of the bird emerged in the pine. It does not matter how you meet a capercaillie in the wild – whether it is hunched comatose in a blizzard like a two-dimensional tea cosy, hurtling hugely into a flight of uncanny control through the thickest trees (and often unnerving a second bird so that the uncanniness is performed in formation) or sounding the earliest of morning alarms above your

89

sleeping bag; it is never a mundane occasion. I have my reservations about anthropomorphism, but there is all the arrogant swagger of a pipe major about a cock caper on his spring lekking ground, and many of the elements of grand opera and high farce in the heavily ritualised delivery of what passes for his song.

The bathwatering, woodpeckering one began parading along his branch, which somehow heightened the illusion of the pipe major, head high, back arched, tail thrown up like a black sunrise. When he finally flew down to strut his stuff on the lekking ground he was a war-painted chief, primed for the fray and the honour and the glory. It is not hard to be anthropomorphic about a capercaillie. There was enough light on him now to catch the colours. He is a giant grouse, the world's biggest – red-wattled, purple-headed, blue-black-throated (neck feathers flared and set like the skin of a pineapple), bottle-green-bellied, and stroppy with it.

In the wrong frame of mind, particularly aggressive birds will face down a roe deer or a human. Records of assaults on people are far from isolated.

I saw snatches of the lek's pageant through screens of juniper. I was fifty yards away from the centre of the action having crawled a dozen yards to the junipers still in my sleeping bag. I dared not move further, but caught the drift of the action from those peripheral activities I could see clearly. There were at least four cocks, leaping and bouncing in miniature flights of a few feet at a time; once a hen bird ran off towards me pursued by a cock which deflected her back into the arena with all the deftness of a working collie; occasionally a mated female mooched slowly away from the rumpus, wearing a dowdy downcast air in contrast with the pipe-majoring squires.

It was over by about seven, the males suddenly scattering fast through the tree tops, circling far out over the glen flashing white-barred wings, a formidable enough formation to unnerve a goosander up from the river into frantic retreat. I followed the birds' circling flights until I lost them in the immensity of mountains which hem that glen's tattered rag of the old pine forest, a remnant of a remnant. The sparseness of the trees which permit the mountains to dominate the landscape so much more than they do in Rothiemurchus, also robbed the capercaillies of their impact in flight. They are immense in the close-knit forest of the west or in glorious Glen Tanar to the east of the Cairngorms; here they dwindle in seconds to dark leaves blowing on the wind, an unfitting exit for the second-best bird spectacle in the pinewoods.

The best has spread its fame far beyond the frontiers of the woods, far beyond the rarified confines of ornithology, to become a superstar of the wilds. There is a school of thought in the Highlands which equates wildlife and landscape conservation with a kind of fossilised Hades in which all development potential is consumed in eternal fires stoked by legions of beards and green wellies. 'We will not', as one doyen of the ski lobby's determination to infiltrate the dotterel breeding grounds above Drumochter once remarked to a journalist, 'be fobbed off by a couple of birds' nests.' Around the Cairngorms, there is a one-word response which detonates the philosophy – 'osprey'.

When the half-hearted migrant birds of the 1930s and 1940s finally consolidated their instincts in the late 1950s and nested in an old Scots pine on Speyside, they set in motion not only the best-chronicled miracle of forgiving ornithological regeneration in the Highlands but also an unprecedented public relations exercise on behalf of birds. Ospreys now dignify much of Strathspey's tourist literature, and what was once an unsung bend in the road called Boat of Garten now greets visitors with a colourful sign proclaiming 'The Osprey Village'. The birds have become the RSPB's Scottish showpiece: thousands trek to the Loch Garten hide every year – a total of well over a million now – and peer optimistically at every big bird silhouette on Speyside thereafter. I know the fascination and the frustration, for of all seasons and landscapes, of all my watching of any bird or beast or flower or fly, nothing I know is as blatantly, heartwarmingly, inexplicably good as the first early spring glimpse of that old familiar wing-wavered silhouette above the Strathspey pines and birches, with the Cairngorms looming hugely behind in the glasses.

From deep in a chaotic old drawer full of newspaper and magazine cuttings, the selective debris of twenty-four years of journalism, I dusted down the tribute which is appropriate here. Without the early guidance and eagerly shared knowledge of the one called 'He Who

Knows', my osprey store might well have been a meagre gleaning instead of a treasure hoard which enriches every year. A ragged cutting begins:

I have watched a fortnight now. The usual time, the usual place, the same old sights and sounds of spring on the loch, the same old mountain skyline, the same old false starts as the big gulls shimmy in mid-flight. You can never tell when the first osprey will turn up, but there is not much point in looking before the last few days of March, and they rarely arrive later than the third week in April. It is one of those dates like Easter, a movable feast, and one which marks resurrections of its own. It is a renewal of the wild faith.

This, however, has been a long, forlorn March-into-April vigil, and confronted only by rising gull and dwindling goose clamours, unconsoled by the dizzy dance of courting grebes, I seek out He Who Knows on the high ground above the osprey loch. He Who Knows and I who know a little less have paid our osprey dues together, lugged our night-weariness up through staggering spring dawns from the eyrie hide to compare notes over breakfast and pronounce new-forming osprey theories. The birds have a hold on the pair of us.

He Who Knows knew. One bird, he said, in this morning, and from the corner of the garden he points to one tree in a couple of square miles of trees. A key in me turns, a cavern stowed with the treasures of the wilds is sprung open.

So Keith Graham – naturalist, broadcaster, writer, friend and fellow-traveller – and I walk down through the same old fields to the same old gate where the fence posts are fieldglass height, and strain willing eyes across duskfuls of forest to a bleached old pine. There sits the prodigal, fresh from Africa, doubtless cursing the demon within him which eats at his migrating soul and drives him north from the sun to night frosts and day sleets and snows. In the half-light, only the white head half a mile away is clearly discernible, but the sight of him is throat-tightening. The wild faith is kept.

Keith and I fall to osprey reminiscences and regurgitations of our own favourite thoughts and theories and moments, and thus while away what for both of us is perhaps the deepest day of spring, walk home to toast it with a glass of the island malt-fire.

I have marked this ritual of the spring migration every year for fifteen years now, and, for reasons which I am slow to acknowledge, accord to the notional reunion with the homecoming osprey an almost reverential significance. At the heart of the ritual is the forgiveness of nature. The nineteenth century's way with ospreys was a relentless regime of persecution which ended in 1899 with their extinction as a breeding species. It is a well documented slaughter, related with some feeling by Adam Watson and Desmond Nethersole-Thompson in their book *The Cairngorms*. The following incident at Loch Morlich in May 1877 was all too typical:

> Booth (Edward Booth, an able naturalist but 'rich, ruthless and obsessional, a man of devious character') cocked his gun and the keeper struck the tree with his stick. 'The female then sprang up and was immediately shot.' This was evidently a very old eyrie, so large, '9 or 10 feet in diameter', that he had not seen the sitting hen's head. In the eyrie there was one egg and fragments of another 'evidently sucked by the grey crows'. So far so good. But the cock was not yet bagged. The keeper now placed Booth and his gun in a rough shelter of branches. 'Just as the men were leaving' the cock returned, but became alarmed and flew away. In less than half an hour it was back and 'flying over afforded an easy shot which brought him down. He dropped part of trout of about ½lb.'

The quotes – apart from the authors' own assessment of Booth – are from Booth's diary.

It took thirty-five years of this century before ospreys prospected again in their old Scottish homeland, and twenty-five years of mixed misfortunes thereafter before breeding became consistent enough to lay the foundations of what has become an increasingly healthy and stable population. What changed? What lured them back? Their pinewood habitat had been ravaged in their absence, after all, by the First World War, and suffered assaults from the Second World War shortly after their return. I think that nature simply forgave and forgot, and fuelled old instincts within wandering birds only with what was suitable about Strathspey. It is nature's kind of timescale – thirty-five years to draw a breath and reconsider, twenty-five more to overwhelm what by then had admittedly become a less determined human resistance. What's sixty years in the lifetime of a species?

The tide of public opinion had also begun to turn, and although the new wave of ospreys still reaped their harvest of outrage (there are still cantankerous remnants who uphold old keeping traditions and still look askance at a hooked beak, preferably along a shotgun barrel), the birds' persistence almost seemed to dare the tide on its new optimistic flow. Seton Gordon inspired a new generation of naturalists, notably Watson and Nethersole-Thompson in the Cairngorms. He must take much of the credit for establishing a climate in which nature writing about all of wild Scotland has won a new and wide readership. The tradition is well served today by a new generation of writers, but I believe that all these writers have simply assisted a process of nature which has the quality of forgiveness at its heart. It still bestows riches on the despoiled Cairngorms, an incomprehensible benevolence. My ritual greeting of the season's first osprey is my acknowledgment.

I had waited half an hour, and a wind of un-springlike ice-fervour made a chilled eternity of that, for all the blue deception of the day. I was more inclined to believe the new snow furring the skyline on both sides of Strathspey and the piled clouds welling wild and black at their backs. Something of sunshine slipped those cloud fetters, though, and I shifted to feel it on my back so that it blunted the wind's saw teeth at the same time, but an osprey-watcher's eyrie is rarely made like that, and soon enough I stopped the useless shifting, shivered on, and just waited. I had waited forty-five minutes and started twice when two big black-backs caught sudden sun-blinks as they shook water from their wings after take-off, but a glance through the glasses calmed me. I was not waiting for gulls.

I had waited fifty-five minutes when a heron came at me head-on. That produced a flutter of heartbeats until it banked and lifted and showed a heron head and trailing legs. I was not waiting for herons. I had waited an hour and ten minutes when a great-crested grebe swam past and looked me in the eye and dived and resurfaced. He dived and resurfaced and dived and resurfaced all the way across to the reeds, which is a long dive away, and that killed another five minutes, but I was not waiting for grebes.

I had waited an hour and twenty minutes when the common sandpipers which had crossed and trilled and cheered my waiting landed three abreast on the waterside branches and fidgeted away a few seconds. But three sandpipers is a crowd at this time of year and they tripped and trilled off on liquorice allsort wings from this bay to that with their beautiful bickerings scattering the water as they flew. But I was not waiting for sandpipers.

I had waited an hour and a half when cormorant commotion erupted. The bird threshed the water and dived and surfaced and stood and fell on its chin, while all the time, the eel it was trying to swallow was being characteristically slippery, and all that killed another five minutes until the eel slipped its last slip, which was down the cormorant's throat. The cormorant's water calmed, but I was not waiting for cormorants.

I stood stiff and cold and stretched and turned my back on the water for the sake of something else to look at, and as I turned to look up, there he was and my waiting was done. He sailed in on long wind-fingering wings at twenty, perhaps thirty feet above my head. The sun picked him up and dazzled the white of him, glossed the black of him and danced on his crown. He stayed for thirty seconds, circling my empty bay. Thirty seconds for two hours might have been a poor exchange for any other thirty seconds, but not these thirty seconds.

For thirty seconds he circled sun-wise and that landscape of white mountain and brown hill and grey-blue water and green-black forest which had held my gaze for two hours became the blurred stage on which he whirled and wheeled. For thirty seconds, sensations and images of springs and summers past crowded into my mind, fighting to be seen and heard and sensed in the face of the supremacy of the real thing fifty yards offshore. When twenty-nine seconds slipped into thirty, he wheeled abruptly and sped with a leisured ease towards the far shore where the water might be calmer and the fishing easier. I lost him against the hill then, but the one thing I knew was that I had not lost him. All the time, it was the homecoming osprey I was waiting for.

I let that Strathspey afternoon slip into its lengthening spring dusk, watching for the osprey's return. Often he comes down to fish in the evening, when – just as often – the wind falls away, the colours soften and subdue, and paying homage to the forgiveness of nature becomes a privilege rather than a penance of wind-knives. Dusk drew hill-grey veils across the water, but no hill grey was ever just grey, and overtones and undertones and inbetweentones of pink and yellow and purple insinuated through what was left of the light. The water settled, stilled, but the flatness of the light smothered the surface with an opaque whiteness so that the water reflected nothing. Land and watersheet sat one on top of the other, as featureless as bad stage props. A trilogy of inked-in ducks vaulted a small headland and came on, water-hugging southwards, vaulted my own shore so close as they passed that their quacked intonations and wing-slashed windsong fell clearly down the still air. In the right time and place, there is magic even in mere mallards.

Then, as far out as the drawn veils allowed the glasses to explore, there was the silhouette I awaited, the familiar wide-winged, shallow-cleaving, head-down style of my hunting osprey. *My* osprey? 'Mine' since that first bleary-eyed sentry duty by a dead eyrie tree, sharing the bird's bustling night forest world, the spring and summer sunrises and dusks. I watched her head-back pantings through her broody ordeals by early summer fire. I started as he cast off abruptly from his night's roosting perch for the new dawn's first fish. I heard her screeched acclamation of his return. I saw her head turning to follow the dog fox's purposeful trot below the tree. I thrilled as she rose on the rim of the eyrie to flex night-chilled muscles, scattering clouds of dew across the face of a low blood-sun, a small rain of ice-fire. My birds by right of familiarity if no other.

It was my third night on the shore in four days with the call of the place on me as it is on the birds. I saw the far-hovering osprey dip a wing, fold both and fall. In his last airborne gesture, he thrust both feet out at the water, threw both wings high above his head, and in that position dealt a terminal crushing blow to the flanks of a fish which would never know the nature of its assailant. Its first struggles would be mysteriously darkened by the blanket of the bird's wings laid flat on the water. There was a small uneasy pause as the bird

17   Lairig Ghru from the south, with Coire Bhrochan

18   Lairig Ghru from the flanks of Carn Eilrig

19   Glen Dee, the southern approach to the Lairig Ghru, Carn a Mhaim in snow

20   The twisting entry to Coire Garbhlach in Glenfeshie

floated, then the threshing prelude to take-off, so sluggish after the stylishness of the stoop. As the waters warred around his struggles, I wished, not for the first time, that I had never read of the huge pike which was hauled from a Highland loch with an osprey skeleton embedded in its back.

But the bird won clear, as it almost always does, and the wings, so shallow and wind-sure in the hunting flight, now carved high and low in a shallow power-climb. A dozen feet above the water he glided for a moment to re-arrange the fish beneath him so that its head faced the way he flew. Then he was into his giant stride and there was nothing the fish could do but die a bemused and ignominious death high above the pinewood.

There is a perch on a dead pine where the bird feeds. Below you will find a few flimsy cast-offs, slivers of scales, for the osprey devours even the bones and discards next to nothing. On a branch you will find the wood bruised and bloodied and stained dark with the lifeblood of the waters. The vigils of the nesting days lie ahead, thirty-six critical days of incubation when the small but insistent army of trophy hunters will risk life and limb and the increasing wrath of the law to steal a clutch of osprey eggs. The chicks are worthless – you cannot train a young bird to fly to the lure when its instincts are migratory.

But the bird is not sure enough yet on the face of the land to thrive unaided – still far below a hundred breeding pairs, still at the mercy of one catastrophic season, and it still takes the hand of man to fend off the hands of other men. Old prejudices die hard, and when it comes to ospreys some of them are very die-hard. The Loch Garten visitors – 71,000 in 1989 – are symptomatic of a turning tide, however, and they make their pilgrimage to shoot nothing but film. They swell the coffers of the RSPB which is at the heart of the human response to the osprey's persistence with its old Scottish pinewood heartland. The bird, once a dark monument to prejudice, is now a symbol of its own instincts, of our own slow-dawning awareness, of the sanctuaries which dwell within the shadow of the pines, and of the forgiveness of nature.

What matters now is the habitat, for if it is safeguarded the ospreys and much else besides will prosper. The worth of that Ice-Age-old

21   The Devil's Point, sentinel of Glen Dee

pinewood heritage has one more eloquent advocate in the osprey's return.

The RSPB has put its money where its increasingly voluble mouth is, to become a substantial Speyside landowner, adding the Abernethy pinewoods in 1988 to their Insh reserve of birchwood and marshland. They have also begun to promote, through their Highland officer Roy Dennis, the idea of a concerted planting programme to join together all the Cairngorms pinewood remnants, so that the mountain massif is encircled once again with pine, as it was centuries ago. The Nature Conservancy Council will tell you that he has simply dusted down an old policy of theirs, but the RSPB's flair for public relations has certainly raised the profile of the idea, whoever had it in the first place. It is not just a bold and visionary argument based on self-evident conservation wisdom. Its value to all wildlife, not just birds, would be immeasurable. Its greatest ingenuity is in its contribution to the social welfare of the Cairngorms communities. It will recreate a demand for forestry skills which have all but become obsolete – silviculture will be practised as opposed to the meagre skills of harvesting which are all that today's definition of plantation forestry demands. This would create jobs for all time. What other industry offers that prospect, and in the Highlands of all places where so many employment opportunities are transitory, and so many more are dependent on weather?

The creation and the subsequent management of a pine forest – and a forest it will truly be, not a collection of woods – of such an extent and with the required sensitivity to the competing needs of recreation, tourism, wildlife and landscape is a vast undertaking. How much more valuable and how much more appropriate it would be than skiing! How much more generous a gesture from man towards the landscape he has so devastated for so long.

Roy Dennis has said that you should not use the term 'forest' unless you can walk all day without emerging from the trees. It is a subjective definition, but a sublime target.

I sit on a heathery bank on the edge of a small clearing in the Dell Wood. It is a small national nature reserve owned by the Nature Conservancy Council, a Scots pine enclave *par excellence*, part of Abernethy Forest which is now owned by the RSPB. It is a warm mid-September afternoon, and although there are big winds in the pine tops and gales dusted snow on the high Cairngorms in the night, only small eddies of cool air reach me here to disturb the pervasive warmth. A steady drizzle of pine needles falls gold on the woodland floor; occasionally one glisters briefly on my writing page. A late bee prospects among the last of the heather bloom, a thin reedy sound cutting across the unbroken undertones of the wind. The bottom three or four feet of a nearby pine are aswarm with ants. The bark is deeply cleft and sculpted, black inches-deep ravines for ant explorers. On the cool shadowed side of the tree, there are no ants at all. We are all, the ants and I, working purposely in the sun. They are as mobile as the wind, I as still as their tree. In the clearing, the grasses have lost all trace of summer green. They too are constantly astir, a tawny-and-orange dance, which frenzies occasionally when a bigger wind dips and hurtles through. Islands of withering heather also stir but they offer more resistance, move to a sluggish measure. Every shade and shape of pine tree is gathered here: trees of great age and infancy and infinite depths of middle age throw shadows at each other. In the wind, the shadows race up and down trunks, in and out along boughs and branches like chasing red squirrels. Studded stands of juniper from knee-high to ten feet hold their shadows more resolutely. Webs glitter in the lowest branches.

I climb to that highest treeline zone of Rothiemurchus where the midwinter wind and the last of the trees compete for every square inch of rock and half-hearted heather. It has been a perpetual warring of the elements since that day unknown years after the retreat of the Ice when the first high pine thrust a daring frond over the lip of the corrie's sheltering headwall and the mountain wind dived down to flatten it. Two hundred feet below the treeline I pause. I stand more or less on the two-thousand-feet contour. The trees here are the highest pines anywhere in the land. I drink in the sun and shelter, I warm to the rare and benevolent impact of native trees in a Scottish mountain corrie. I watch the trees fall away like dark waterfalls to the lochs and the strath below. It is a restful thing to do because the trees fit. I climb on through the treeline, into walls of wind. Trees after a fashion still grow, but in their first encounters with the mountain winds they crouch and spread. A pine and a juniper grow side by side, each a foot

high and four feet wide, curved and bristled as hedgehogs. The wind
is the great leveller of the Cairngorms. All life is subservient to it.
Climb enough, look hard enough, find willows less than an inch high
and moss which outgrows them. I turn from the wind and look back
across the pinewoods' only natural limitation. I think how the trees
honour a sense of place in a way which plantation forestry never can.
The lower birchwoods of the Cairngorms' fringes achieve the same
wild poise which trees anywhere only win if they are appropriate. Far
up Strathspey I can pick out the pine forest of Abernethy, where
the pines stand tall and straight as Chelsea Pensioners on Maundy
Thursday, and defer to a small September clearing in the Dell Wood.

There is so much between Creag Fhiaclach of Rothiemurchus and
the Dell Wood of Abernethy which denies the wild poise, the sense of
place. The commercial artery of the Cairngorm road runs through the
heart of it, through plantation-stifled Glen More. If that gap in the old
pine forest can be bridged first it will serve a threefold purpose. First,
it will unite the two finest pinewood remnants, and ensure their
perpetuity. Second, it will impose a pinewood domain on the
maximum number of people, for the Glenmore road is the first
thoroughfare of tourism in the Cairngorms. With thought and care,
opportunities can be seized to convince thousands of visitors a year of
the pinewoods' worth. Third, it will create a wood which, by Roy
Dennis's definition at least, we could call a forest.

Many generations of people have presided over the demise of the
pine forest over so many centuries. But ours is the first to preside over
it while we also preach the worth of our heritage. The governments
of the tropical rain forest countries might take more seriously our
own rebuke at their desecration of that great treasury of the earth if
we showed a commitment to saving our own native forests.

We know the legacy which grows here. Steven and Carlisle offered
three reasons for safeguarding the future of the pines in *The Native
Pinewoods of Scotland*:

First, they are the authentic home of the distinctive strain of Scots
pine at the western extremity of its natural distribution ...
Secondly, the native pinewoods are one of the most interesting
survivals of our native vegetation ... There is now general

recognition in all civilised countries that such survival should be preserved on an adequate scale and it would be a national loss if these pinewoods were allowed to disappear . . . Finally they can be considered to be not the least important of the historical monuments of Scotland . . .

Sit an hour in the Dell Wood or cling with the wind-tormented trees on Creag Fhiaclach and ask yourself if we dare preside over the pinewoods' extinction.

8

Beyond the Shadow

I ACKNOWLEDGED the last pine tree in Gleann Einich with a nod and a small wave. I have no idea where the particular gesture originated, and only half an idea of its significance for me, but it is ritually re-enacted with each and every passing, the crossing of one of nature's frontiers. It has something to do with nourishing the bond between man and landscape, of establishing a benevolent presence in the mind of the landscape.

I am aware that owning up to such a belief, or at least a code of conduct which acknowledges such a thing as the mind of a landscape, is to invite more derision than discipleship. If, however, you trek into the same wild country again and again, seeking intimate acquaintance with a handful of summits, glens, corries, even individual trees and deer and dippers, so that you are recognisable in their midst, you need a different yardstick from the scatter-gun philosophy of the Munro-bagger. If you will pursue the Hill's secrets, nature insists on some conditions of entry – a care and sensitivity in its company, a demonstrable sense of kinship, a respect for wildness, a recognition of the rights of landscape for its own sake.

The *raison d'être* of the Cairngorms is not to balance the books of Highland business and bureaucrats, or to provide councillors and MPs with an opportunity of scoring political points by exploitation for employment. It is not to permit the Countryside Commission for Scotland to 'encourage people to enjoy' the countryside. (There is no reason to 'encourage' people into the countryside, particularly as such encouragement almost invariably amounts to a diluted and artificial introduction to nature. Too much has already been tamed all across Britain under the pretext of 'encouraging people to enjoy'. Besides, be warned that the Cairngorms offer no guarantee that you will enjoy what you find there. Mostly, I do enjoy, but I know others who do not, who find the scale of the place intimidating, the landforms dull.) The true purpose of the Cairngorms is simply to be, to exist in all their glories, and to nurture those distinctive wildlife communities which crave their Arctic-ness.

If there is a value in all that for people, it is in the spiritual and physical benefits they can derive as individuals from such wildness. Seton Gordon wrote the following after a memorable day on Creag an Leth-choin, the Lurcher's Gully of much controversy as the ultimate target of Cairngorm's skiing developers:

> One was reluctant to leave the high tops on an evening such as this. In the immense silences of these wild corries and dark rocks, the spirit of the high and lonely places revealed herself, so that one felt the serene and benign influence that has from time to time caused men to leave the society of their fellows and live on some remote surf-drenched isle – as St Cuthbert did on Farne – there to steep themselves in those spiritual influences that are hard to receive in the crowded hours of human life.

Skiing development in the Cairngorms has since transplanted the crowded hours of human life into the kingdom of this spirit of the high and lonely places. Whether you believe that these things are absorbed by a landscape 'mind' or not, the wandering individual will always find it difficult to resist the acknowledgment of a creative force within wildest nature to which he and his purpose are subservient.

I tramped out beyond the shadow of the pines through deepening snow into that Cairngorms realm of moorland and long, wide glens, foothills and mountain flanks, relishing at once the sense of a freer, deeper winter. Black clouds massed over the Moine Mhor, that high plateau which sprawls away from the top of Gleann Einich's 'cul-de-sac' headwall. The sun fitfully blazed and snuffed daring spotlights so that the glen's mountain walls were never still, never uniformly white, but every subtle shade of dark white and pale white and sullen grey.

The river had begun to narrow yard by yard as the stranglehold of ice and heaped snow banks encroached. I paused to watch the light's dance, decided on a brew, and as the stove wheezed I became preoccupied with a dipper's unflinching zeal, perching on an iced rock to sing, swimming and diving down through the current – more ice than water – to feed after its own perversely amphibious fashion on the riverbed. Is there a grittier gladiator-of-the-wilds than the dipper, I wondered, at which point there was a tiny scuffling inches away from my feet, and a determined busy-ness under the overhanging lip of the snow's newly redefined riverbank. It was a wren.

There are times when nature's logic is incomprehensible. There is no common species of bird in Britain more susceptible to winter harshness than the wren, no winter climate harsher in Britain than the Cairngorms. We – the wren and I – were three miles out beyond the pinewoods, both of us heading determinedly upstream, the wren foraging with some success in the very jaws of winter. Wrens, like long-tailed tits, fend off the worst of winter in communal roosts, and there are many records of crowds of wrens packed into tiny improvised shelters, including the tragic failures – forty dead in a nest box. It seems nothing more than a tidy way to die. So why this single bird speck on the winter face of the Cairngorms?

The coffee brewed, the wren busied on upstream, the plateau wind whipped away the towers of cloud and the sun won an unfettered hour. I was still turning over the wren conundrum, wondering what it feels like to delve into those icily sodden overhangs and pluck a spider from the white darkness, when my dawdling glance fastened on the unquestionable silhouette of a golden eagle high over Carn Eilrig. The great bird (why 'great', and in the circumstances was he any greater than this wren?) flew south-west out over the glen on unbeaten wings (the wren's were a restless blur), then, as I locked the glasses on to him, launched into the matchless aerobatic routine of his display flight. The eagle's roller-coastering would tilt the whole Cairngorms landmass into yawning skylines, the rush of air about his flawless streamlinings a heady roar, the hard climb back up the spilled air a turbocharging sequel to the momentum of the free-fall, power-driven beyond the comprehension of mere mortals, beyond the consciousness of wrens. The performance marked that critical point in the wild cycle of the eagle which announces an end to the old year, the bird convinced despite the day's snows and the river's ice that winter has frayed beyond repair. A commitment is launched to a sustained expenditure of energy which will last half a year, beginning with this stylised sky-dance.

Eagle eyries can be immense even by the standards of the rarified world of eagle statistics, and in the Cairngorms, where tree-nesting is still a fairly regular occurrence, they can assume the proportions of nature's answer to the Scottish tower house. Seton Gordon described one in his book, *The Golden Eagle*:

> This eyrie, to my personal knowledge, has been in use during a period of forty-five years. It has gradually increased in size until (1954) it is approximately fifteen feet deep. The top of the eyrie is now actually the highest part of the tree. Looking at this eyrie from the ground, the observer sees how one nest after another has been built on the foundations of the last, and that each eyrie retains its individuality in the whole structure. The brooding eagle must now be prepared to face much exposure. The weight of this great eyrie must be a burden to the old fir, yet it remains erect and sturdy at the age of perhaps 300 years while others around it have been over-thrown by winter gales . . .

The rigours of the construction process, mating, brooding, rearing the eaglets, fetching and carrying prey which can be as large as a dog fox or a deer calf (as pitifully meagre as a mouse or vole on wearying lean days), teaching the young the phenomenal skills of eagle flight – all these amount to an exacting routine performed in the face of the harshest mountain climate in the land. It is a routine for which only eagles are fitted, and its beginning served, after the encounter with the wren, to demonstrate something of the scale of nature's repertoire which is required to fulfil the demands of the ecology of a single hillside. There can be few more telling extremes of the wilds with which to confront and convince your sensibilities than the golden eagle predator and the prey of a wren on the same hillside.

On that same late February day on that same late February hillside, the wren was scavenging scraps of survival three thousand feet below the celebrating eagle. Even now, a hard week of frosts or prolonged snows could prove fatal for a tiny bird so weakened by winter. Yet when winter relents sufficiently, the wren may well nest higher than the eagle. There is nothing rare about wren nests at two thousand feet, even though they may be more familiar in your back garden. The eagle, particularly the tree-nester, often nests several hundred feet lower. There will be times when a boulder-singing wren pauses in mid-chorus to cast a wary eye *down* on the formidable back and wingspan of an eagle bearing home a haunch of deer carrion or a brace of ptarmigan.

The kind of familiarity I have won with this hillside by many explorations in every season and weather is a puny reckoning in this company. It is puny even by the standards of other people who went before, the shieling folk who lived in the glen for months at a time. How many naturalists of unconscious genius whiled away the heart of the year watching over cattle in a glen like this? How close to the land and the animal state they must have been, and how respectful of the land, because they knew that to abuse it would be to upset the fine balance which sustained their quality of life. Yet how little knowledge even they must have accumulated in a lifetime compared to the wren's store! To spend every waking hour scouring the nooks and crevices and crannies of the lower half of the mountain, the glen floor, the burn's fluctuating banks, in pursuit of all that hillside's crawling and flying minutiae is to *know* the place. There is a greater depth to the wren's knowledge than that, however, for it must balance its loud voice and conspicuous way with a rock podium against its vulnerability as prey. There is none of the meadow pipit's discretion about a wren. So it must also have an eye for every fold and furrow and bluff and boulder which might conceal the soft-shoe approach of a fox, or the swift low dart of a hunting hawk. For the most part, the wren's will be a heather-low-boulder-high familiarity, but think what its accumulated knowledge of three or four winters and summers could teach science about the teeming underfoot lives of a Cairngorms hillside. And when he rises to perch and proclaim his patch of spring and summer hill, does the cock's eye ever follow the dipper's speculative flights up to the plateau or even scan the skies for the impossibly high eagle?

At six thousand feet, the wren's glen is a flattened trough, its watersheets glittering droplets like beads of sweat on the palms of the land. The eagle sees not just the unified nature of the Cairngorms landmass – it sets it in its widest context midway between Scotland's shores. The movement of a wren from rock perch to heather depths may not be discernible, but the eagle will mark the movement of deer, the purposeful trot of the red fox across the hill flanks, the counter-march of hares, the freewheeling winter blizzard of flocked ptarmigan down the corrie walls, the herds of people in Corrie Cas, the trekkers in almost every corner of the landscape. On a day of late March or early April, the eagle sees the shallow-winged flight of another big hook-beaked bird driving forcefully north up the Spey trailing a wake of enraged crows, and knows that the fish-hunter is back from his winter wanderings. The land I tramp in solitude is a teeming place in the eye of the eagle.

I watched him climb tinily high until he simply climbed beyond the range of the naked eye. I found him again with the glasses, hurtling towards the plateau, saw him level off and dive again, level and dive, until he was carving down the air of my own hillside. He pulled out at about two thousand feet, and rose to a high rock perch on the upper rim of a corrie, and there he sat, doubtless digesting the exhilaration of the flight. Two hours later, after I had delved into the glen's whitest depths and returned, he was still there, and another of my own limitations in the company of eagles was reinforced. To sit quite still for two hours at three thousand feet in the snow wind of late February and do nothing – and for all I know sit there for another two hours – is beyond my reach. To be to all intents and purposes a piece of the mountainside, a fragment of the Cairngorms landscape, immo-bile as granite, is to achieve a bonded closeness with the landscape which is not given to humans, or at least not to today's generations. There were old intimacies, such as that shown by the Eskimos' copious vocabulary to deal with different kinds of snow in differing conditions, though this too has dwindled. The Eskimo definition of the Arctic has suffered approximately similar fates to those which have befallen the Cairngorms definition of Arctic. Wilderness is in retreat the world over in parallel with our sensitivity towards it and our awareness of its worth.

I began my return journey down the glen with a high rambling detour contouring the hillside where the autobiographical trivia of fox and hare and deer are imprinted on the snows, along the gullies of snow-buried burns, always pursuing the spoor of the natives, trying to decode the symbolism of the tracks. Here was a hare, ambling along in placid sets-of-four tracks, and here is where it suddenly thrust its hind feet deep and kicked into an uphill sprint, drawing the tracks out into elongated yard-long strides. There is no hint of pursuit in the snow, its enemy was not fox, or climber's dog intoxicated by the hill air and the gamey scent. Eagle? After fifty yards, here is where the hare paused and sat (I see him rise on his hind legs, ears erect, nose working the wind which brings the scent of fear or the merciful reassurance of scentlessness). Here is where, suitably reassured, the hare dropped to all fours again and resumed his leisurely gait.

Two foxes have been out, their single file tracks keeping their distance, occasionally crossing each other, twice meeting in a crumpled strewment of snows. Eager contact, or conflict?

That is the way I love to pass my time in the mountains, rummaging the contours, encircling a hill, crossing watersheds, hugging burns, sitting for as long as my un-eagle tolerances will permit. It conveys something of wildlife's slant on the ground, the one from which we can learn most, the one which should shape our thinking about how we treat the Cairngorms. Only wildlife *needs* to use this landscape, and only this of all our landscapes can fulfil the needs of some of the most specialised wildlife. Adam Watson and Desmond Nethersole-Thompson make the point well in the introduction to their 'Hill Birds' chapter of *The Cairngorms*:

Birds on the high Cairngorms are thus more like the birds of the Arctic tundra than the hill birds of the European Alps. This Arctic affinity is no surprise as it is also true of invertebrates, vegetation, climate, soil, topography and the appearance of the landscape. The main affinities of our hill birds with the Arctic are: ptarmigan are common on most of the hill ground . . . snow buntings breed in a few places, dotterel nest on many high grasslands and a snowy owl has frequented the Ben Mac Dhui plateau in several years. All four are species whose world distribution is mainly Arctic or sub-Arctic . . .

What marks the Cairngorms' significance in terms of such birds is the *scale* of suitable habitat. It is the vastness of the Arctic landscape which appeals to its indigenous wildlife, not simply the fact of enough space to defend a single territory.

I came down to the wren's mainstream burn again, and paused a cold half-hour just beyond the embrace of the first of the pinewoods. From a lowly elevation above the glen floor I could trace all my day's journey, out over the wide moorland, deep into the throat of the glen, back along the shelves and flanks of the glen's hillsides. I found that I had spent seven hours without leaving a glen I could walk through in less than two, and without climbing higher than about two thousand feet. I had spent a third of one of those hours with the eagle, but otherwise had seen nothing more exotic than a wren and a dipper, and the aftermath of fox and hare jaunts.

There are those who would regard that as a poor return for a day spent in these mountains, but such days have less definable rewards, more durable too than the ticking off of one more summit. There is, I think, within the physical framework of the land, a terrain of the mind, a spiritual journey which can enrich the physical experience of being in wild places, or – as in the example of that dire January afternoon in the grey depths of the pinewood – impoverish it. What it does is to intensify the scope of response to the landscape at both extremes of the emotional range. Sensitivity to wildness grows more profound. I will stitch many such days together in any one Cairngorms year and call none of them dull, for I hold their accumulated value as something priceless.

Our own era's preoccupation with scientifically irrefutable truths breeds contempt for the spiritual landscape. So does the tendency towards collecting summits, wearing achievement badges, the imposition of 'outdoor education' on the school syllabus like algebra. The process is assisted by the marketing of gaudy mountain clothing and equipment which actually oppose the concept of a closeness with the land. Guidebooks which spell out every detail, dot and comma of a route deny the exercise of judgment and the joy of discovery. The relentless erosion of the Scottish mountain tradition at the hand of bureaucracies rooted in alien cultures and committee management is just as lethal.

The land is the one ultimate security we have, the ultimate endurable, the highest art form in our world. Where there is still land of such exclusive wildness as the Cairngorms, we should set it aside, purposefully but without fuss, so that its wildness flourishes unhindered.

As I turned to walk back down through the trees, a last hour of sunlight flooded the forest. A small group of red deer hinds and calves stood at ease in the nearest pines, sheltered from the wind, drinking in the sun's spring-like promise. The day had begun in midwinter and now contrived an illusion at least of a new season. We, the deer and I, were grateful but not impressed. They, of all creatures, know the landscape repertoire of winters for all seasons. By midnight it was minus three, and by dawn it was snowing again. A wren danced drably up the burn in the first light.

I was back in the glen a week later, and in the intervening days winter had retreated far up the mountain. The burn rang with the dash of meltwaters and its banks were things of substance again – grass, heather, peat, rock. The new song of mistle thrushes followed me far out across the moor from the woods. The deer were further out, feeding eagerly on the moor turned soft and brown again after the week-long thaw. I counted almost two hundred beasts scattered along the moorland shelf under the mountain walls, the nearest of them in two groups of thirty or forty, divided by a gully and its burn and its ice-hard old snow wedges.

I dropped into the gully, splashed softly upstream between head-high heathery banks, hauled myself out about eighty yards from the nearest beast. There I lay in the heather, and watched and listened. The windlessness of the spot was almost warm, although there were little more than glimmers of sun. I basked in the hour's tranquillity, and sensed something of the same attitude in the deer. Days like these must be as restorative for the deer as they are for people. There is the temptation to believe that the back of winter is broken. Your ear attunes to the long-lost thrush-song, you peel off an outer layer of windproof clothing. There will be late snows and late frosts and late winds – there always are hereabouts, and some of them are very late – but the ferocity of winter's onslaught at least is on the ebb.

Spring is the deer's wound-licking season. There is the cost of winter to be counted in a land where too many deer find the season's meagre grazing too poor. Too many pines will have died in the futile cause of trying to make ends meet for the deer. Too many deer lie as bleaching skeletons, monuments to the old season, but by their deaths a handful of other hill tribes have survived – eagle, buzzard, raven, crow, fox, scavengers all. Ahead for the survivors and winter's war-wounded lie the rigours of calving (and the renewed attentions of eagles), the uneasy demise of summer and the autumn rut, by which time a new winter will have sounded more than one warning blast.

These days of notional early spring are good days to come close to the red deer, to see them strung out and relaxed, the hinds and last year's young in their markedly redder coats muttering and barking. It makes for fascinating eavesdropping, trying to fathom meaning from their sounds. The vocabulary to human ears seems a restricted one, but beyond that there are other channels of communication.

In my mind was an incident of a month earlier as I walked down the same glen near the limit of the pines. I came suddenly on an old hind on a small knoll above the track. Below her, a screen of trees obscured my vision further down the glen, and before she retreated uphill she turned to stare not at me but at something behind the trees. Her ears flicked forward, her body tensed as though she was making an intense physical effort. Moments later, four more hinds and three calves emerged from beyond the screening trees, running purposefully in the opposite direction from the line of retreat she now followed. Had she sent them away by alerting them to my presence which they could neither see nor scent? If she had, she had done so without uttering a sound.

Now, in the process of trying to improve my view from the burn's gully, I dislodged a small rock and sent it over the bank and into the water. It made a soft splash, but it brought the head of an old grey matriarch hind whirling up and round. No other deer flinched. Was she the appointed sentry under whose vigilance the other younger deer relaxed? Or had only she heard, sensed perhaps, with the sensitivity exclusive to her experience? She looked hard at me, then at the other deer. Again, no sound, but one by one the heads came up to meet her gaze, caught the drift of her alarm and focused on me. The alarm crossed the burn, and within moments a tawny stain of retreating deer was drifting south along the hillside, two hundred beasts mobilised without a sound.

It was an easy retreat, for a calm space has opened in the year of the deer. The matriarch marks it just as surely as the free-falling eagle marks his change, and she will nurse its lifeline of hope and expectancy through the lessening assaults of winter (these will include such as that May blizzard which cut the glen off from all its watersheds for a week, when the young pregnant hinds grew fearful, but she nursed that dark smothering white hour away too, she's seen it all) . . .

If you walk up the sheltered side of the hill, go early. The bracken is an infernal, fly-stifled cloying sea of green whirlpools which clutch at your legs, your waist, your chest if you go deep enough in. Early enough, you can foil the fly hordes which like the sun on their backs as they ply their wretched droner's trade. If you can't go early, my best advice is to be a whinchat.

The white-splashed buff and brown of him sways a breeze-bowed frond, then leaps to flay the hordes by the beakful (you learn to pray through the high summer for a plague of whinchats because of the toll they take on the flies, but there are never enough). The flaying done he drops back to a heavy-footed landing on the same frond, bows it more respectfully lower than ever, rides the straightening rise of the plant. Then, Spitfire-winged, he slips on to the breeze briefly and ducks down to a small six-beaked sanctuary of moss and grass weavings. The beaks yawn yellow, the white eye-stripes stab down into each beak, the beaks fill and empty, and he is gone with a dull pastel flourish.

As he goes, he spares less than a glance for the small heap of white-spotted bright-brown something-or-other where it lies, a graceful slump of long-limbed hooves and long-lashed black eyes, an uncanny assembly of curves and angles, arches and spindles, the delicate geometry of high summer's red deer calf. She is two days old. She looks a forlorn abandoned waif, which is the crude human judgment that so often accounts for her downfall. She is none of these. Follow that newly-trod twin-slotted trail through the bracken to the high ground and you'll find a watchful hind browsing and listening and watching. Sit high and still and watch her thread back down the trail to kiss and caress and console her couched calf, and if the breeze stills and you can be close enough and stay unseen, hear the soft-tongued small-talk of the red deer nursery.

But for all the attentions of her mother and the helping hands of the other hinds and the vigilance of the matriarch, these are dangerous days for the calf. A big deer-watching dog fox will take her, and an ill-judged movement will betray her to the high cruising eagle. Some keepers, still determined that yesterday's prejudices will die hard in the face of today's enlightened research, will tell you stories of eagles and red deer calves to make less honest men blush, and the only thing anyone knows for sure about such encounters is that no one knows for sure how often eagles take calves. For the strongest bird, the slightest calf is a considerable burden, the attentions of the hind often vicious, so if there is an easier prey among the slow-flying ptarmigan or the scree-bolting hare – even an unwary fox cub, which is the one the game-keeper would rather not tell you about – the eagle will look there first, and take carrion before any of these. The easier the meat, the better. Life is hard enough without daring the hooves of infuriated hinds.

A bigger threat to the bundle by the whinchat's nest is the two-legged oaf who stumbles on her, sees the Bambi-esque waif, and gathers the beast into his arms to dump on a convenient friend who mends sparrowhawk wings in his spare time. The result is either a suffering death or a life of captivity instead of freedom, and there is not a wild beast or bird alive or dead who would have chosen that.

So if you climb the brackeny hill and find yourself sucked down into one of those green whirlpools where a small heap of bright-brown white-spotted something-or-other lies low, leave it be. It's you who's lost . . .

The matriarch marks a second change. The calves are running sturdily, the brief summer is done, the first frosts sharpen the night air, the first snows whisper about the summits. September wearies, silver birches grow gold. The mountain is restless . . .

. . . Something in the bog-myrtled air drops a hint of a happening. Through the glasses, I pick out two stags, young, well-shouldered, autumn-sheened, ready. There is a sudden unprovoked bickering, a gesture of lowered heads and flourished antlers, a steady advance, a thoughtful retreat, a point proved. Not the real thing, not yet, but a hint of things to come. A trickle of stones licks down the mountain-side beneath the stags' stamping feet, precursor of the passion ava-lanche of the rut.

Something slows my stride in the deer glen at this season, a thing of hill spirits to which a far-flung Celtic ancestry has left me susceptible, for to ponder the red deer domain from within as its society subtly reshapes and regroups for the rut is to dwell on the ways of more than mere hill beasts. The red deer are the faery cattle of the Gael, the hinds hand-milked in faery dawns. The eternal Celtic twilight of half-fact and half-legend (often much corrupted by modern invention!) has coloured centuries of human life in lands like these. Clan rituals, stalkers' encounters, the solitary wanderings of hill gangrels have all been touched by such impenetrable mists. It is while you sit through these last uneasy overtures to the rut, contemplating the new con-fidence of the young stags and the head of the old master stag grey with doubt but awesome with pride, that the Hill is inclined to unveil its most seductive half-truths. Come the rut itself there is little of contemplative silence, for its bellowed passions delve deep even into the sanctuary of the mountain night; after the rut, there is winter to contend with, an infertile season for mysticism. For now, however, while the faery light shines and the hill mind is willing, legend crowds round. There are many, many stories, and I have heard a few from the unlikeliest of dour-faced sources. Often I believe, however, and where I do not I sympathise. I have a story of my own.

I had come to a rock chair high above the watershed, sat and stilled. The morning had emerged Landseer-shrouded, unfathomably grey, the hill grasses a sodden tawny understorey which fell away to cloud-shuttered glens. Sounds and scents melted weirdly with mists and sodden air to paint the wildest masterpiece of all the Highland's repertoires. For a long hour I peered down into the western gloom of the glen, secure in the west wind buffeting my scent far out over the crags to the east, while the hoarse song of the rut danced to the wind's tune about the rock walls. A kestrel wheeled and fretted down on the dipping land, working the wind, a poised pirate. He planed along the crags, stood off my own rock for perhaps ten seconds, then he fell, checked, fell again, checked, and finally thumped softly into the grasses where he so closely matched the autumn colours that it looked as if the hill had reclaimed its own temporarily dislodged fragment, like a golfer replacing a divot.

He rose, vole-taloned, cut away east on the wind, and I redirected eyes and ears to the deer.

It began to rain. The nearest action of the rut seemed to have drifted off across the hillside, so that I gleaned only echoings now. The proximity of the kestrel, the cloak of the rains and the lowering of the cloudbase turned me in on myself, and may have contributed to my perception of what happened next.

The fall from grace of an old master stag is the saddest parting of the autumn mists. He barged through the cloying curtain, peat-blackened, grey-muzzled, rut-bloodied, to the watershed directly beneath me. He was going east when the rut was west, fleeing the arena of triumphant youth, the monarch dethroned. He was too heavy, too slow, too old, and too proud to let his exit go unnoticed. He turned his great grey neck to the west while his torso faced unflinchingly east, and poured a wild contempt across the glen in one appalling roar. But the wind would blunt its message, baulk its journey and dissipate its power into a thousand blown splinters of sound.

It is rare to see nature at its most ruthlessly logical. It is a raw precept which protects the species yet dismisses the individual so callously, banished into the corrie of the exile. I wished him a brief and placid exile, but the faery folk are good to their own and know the worth of mercy.

Then, on an impulse, I took a scrambling detouring descent down the crag to close on the stag and watch his own descent to the east, his enactment of the inevitable wild ritual. He was twenty yards away when I came to the lee of a rock and put the glasses on him. He stepped beyond a rise in the ground and I followed. His tracks gleamed wetly on a yard of deer track among the rocks, but when I inched round it, still screened by the wind, and having primed the camera in anticipation of a close-quartered encounter, there was nothing. The track led down into a wide bowl of grass and rock. Nothing. The rock piled massively behind and above. Impossible. As

I watched, the clouds threw back from the corrie walls and the sun speared down. There was no hiding place for a stag within any distance it might reasonably have covered in the time it had been out of sight. I sat another uneasy half-hour, scouring the corrie again and again, and arriving again at the same eerie, reluctant conclusion. The stag had vanished into the wind-whipped corrie air.

The kestrel suddenly dipped back into its midst and poised patiently there, reasserting my grip on the realities of the last hour. There had been a kestrel. There had been a stag. Now there was only the dangling falcon and a chill which had emerged with the sun.

There will be scoffers, but there will be others who may nod quietly, because such things will have happened to them. Still others will present easy answers and sniffy dismissiveness. But if you have read and talked and sat and seen and listened and wondered, if you have sensed the chill unease, you may concede at least that when the Cairngorms muster their moodiest seductions the red deer may inhabit a domain which is not exclusively nature's.

9

A Repertoire of Corries

I HAD CLIMBED in pursuit of the rut into the lowest and least of the mountain's corries, little more than a denting of the contour lines, a crow's nest to spy on the glen, a place from which to cast an eager eye upwards to headier corrie heights. At their highest and mightiest they are among the chieftains of the Cairngorms' landscape glories. They puncture the fabric of the mountain massif with the whorls of a mighty clutch of thumbprints. Up there you are far beyond the shadow of the pines. The shadows which darken those innermost fastnesses of winter's kingdom are the shadows of the total mountain itself.

By mid-November, it had been snowing steadily in the high Cairngorms for a week. 'Snowing steadily' may suggest that limpid, pretty snow of Christmas card farmyards, the kind of snow in which you are happy for your children to play. On the Cairngorms plateau at four thousand feet, the snow often travels sideways at sixty miles an hour, gusts to a hundred, and it hurts. In the corries such winds go berserk, pouring over headwalls, dizzying around the sidewalls, skating as whirlwinds across the high watersheets such as Loch Etchachan under Ben Mac Dhui, and setting up so many collisions of air currents that a blizzard becomes a nightmare. To be in such places at such times is to learn more forcibly than words can ever convey that you shouldn't be. Ground and sky and landscape become meaningless, colour and visibility belong to other days and circumstances, navigation becomes a terrifyingly exact science.

Yet all you will see of it from the valleys of Spey or Dee is its grey shroud, the mountain mass severed at two thousand feet, the summits invisible for a week, and only the race of detached scraps of cloud across the sky to suggest the frantic turmoil within the shroud.

Then the whole thing relents for a day, the shroud begins to shred into a fractured mass which apes the shapes of the mountain massif, and suns and mountainous clouds do battle. Mountain shoulders will bare briefly, seductively white. On such a relenting day, Cameron McNeish and I wandered deep into Glen Feshie to admire the work of the snows. Mostly I climb and wander alone. If I have company, I prefer company like Cameron's for his like-minded attitude to these mountains. We are brothers of the same hill-going tradition and seek much the same solaces in the Cairngorms.

We put the moorland tramp behind us and dropped into the baffling folds of Coire Garbhlach, baffling because, although the initial embrace of the place suggests a more modest Lairig Ghru, the walls confound your distant gaze by bending at right angles every few hundred yards, leaving you to wrestle with an immense geometry of conflicting diagonals. We paused for coffee by the burn and slipped at once into an easy exchange of hillgoing philosophies. At one point Cameron said, 'It's the being that matters. That's what it's all about.' As a sentiment, it was a respectful nod towards the late Nan Shepherd whose slim volume *The Living Mountain* is a hymn to the Cairngorms, a well-thumbed bible for people of our persuasion. Its concluding chapter is simply entitled 'Being' and its last paragraph reads:

> I believe that I now understand in some small measure why the Buddhist goes on pilgrimage to a mountain. The journey is itself part of the technique by which the god is sought. It is a journey into Being; for as I penetrate more deeply into the mountain's life, I penetrate also my own. For an hour I am beyond desire. It is not ecstasy, that leap out of the self that makes man like a god. I am not out of myself, but in myself. I am. To know Being, this is the final grace accorded from the mountain.

It is a sentiment in which I find one small flaw. The *final* grace should be accorded *to* the mountain, so that through that magical attainment of Being you finally recognise and come to terms with the *mountain's* Being.

Coire Garbhlach is the perfect thoroughfare for such philosophi-
sing, for if you have already tramped decades of your own across the
face of the hills' millennia, here is a crash refresher course in all the
crucial elements of the Cairngorms.

It began for us with that easy walk up the burn, relaxed enough to
pronounce our deepest convictions within earshot of the mountain
gods (if you hold to such deities – such gods as I own up to I find in
such places, such religion as I permit within my life I fashion from
granite or gabbro or some such kingdom of the wild winds). A snow
bunting stole our thunder briefly, lilting up over the boulders,
spinning away on the wind as it gained height, the spinning itself a
clue to the waiting mountain weather above: the clouds were high
and fast, and deep into the second twist of the corrie we had just begun
to leave the faintest tread on the night's snow. We watched the snow
bunting go and marvelled aloud at the guts and audacity these birds
brandish as a way of life, and their capacity to gladden beleaguered hill
spirits so that in any of the four Cairngorms winters (elsewhere
known as winter, spring, summer, autumn) you can fumble blizzard-
blind through boulderfields and scatter a handful or a score or a
hundred of them from under your feet, singing as they go.

I slipped into my favourite snow bunting script. I had put a long
hill day behind me, and as I wandered down the evening glen, almost
drunk with the sun and snow and untroubled skies, I saw a large flock
of snow buntings wheeling across the lower glen. I put the glasses on
them, counted to two hundred, then in a wider sweep of the glasses
realised that the flock was the head of an unbroken mass of birds
which stretched for more than a quarter of a mile. I took to the bed of
the burn, using its sound and its banks to cloak my approach, settled
into the lee of a boulder as the first of the flock crossed fifty yards
ahead. The conversation of the flock was a roar of soprano whispers. I
checked my watch and began to count. Twelve hundred birds later,
they had gone; the whole flock took two and a half minutes to pass
my rock. The sight and the sound of it all can still swim dizzily back
into mind at chance encounters with snow buntings. It is a brightly
burning torch I carry for the white sparrows . . .

Coire Garbhlach lurched right again, the song of its snow-fuelled
waterfall underscored by a percussive repetitive flatulence in the rocks

above. We muttered 'ptarmigan' in much the same breath, but saw nothing, climbed another leg of the twisting corrie and paused again when the belching rang out just above our heads. I primed the camera and took a wide scrambling detour up the schisty flanks of the corrie to come on the birds from above and behind with Cameron reporting their response – an increasing edginess – from below. I eased round the last intervening rock to find two craning heads not six feet away, too close for the long lens I had fitted. My reward was an eyeball encounter with two cock birds in new ermine, vivid white bar the black of the tail's tip and the eye stripe, the blood red of the wattle. They were crouched low as tortoises, but as our eyes met they both stood tall in unison, a perfectly turned out double act of nature's choreography. There are few birds which change shape quite so dramatically as the ptarmigan with its instantaneous transformation from low flattened crouch to stretch-necked sentry. In winter plumage it is a flawless, dazzling moment to witness at such a distance.

Ptarmigan is the Arctic grouse. The head and neck have a vaguely reptilian air, particularly when you catch the bird craning at you round a rock which obscures its body. Thick-feathered feet work like snow shoes. The seasons' comings and goings are mirrored by a series of partial moults, an uncanny ritual of camouflage, but with the Cairngorms climate and sparse vegetation to contend with, as well as the neighbourhood eagles, the ptarmigan needs every scrap of nature's compassionate assistance. Only the worst of the weather drives the birds below 2,500 feet, and if that 'worst' happens to be a nesting season blizzard the birds may desert their eggs with disastrous consequences for the breeding population. Adam Watson, who has studied the birds for much of his life and contributed many distin-guished scientific papers about every aspect of their fascinating way of life and death, has recorded a nest at 4,150 feet. He has also noted that (although up to ten eggs are laid) 'in the Cairngorms the number of young per adult is often 0·3 or less, sometimes 0·1 or even 0·0 . . . ' There are no immunities in the high Cairngorms, even for a creature as supremely adapted as the ptarmigan.

My fingers were suddenly feeling the cold, and as I ransacked the rucksack for mitts I caught sight of the corrie headwall for the first time – the topography of the corrie saves it for the last spectacular eastward twist. The highest rocks wore massive armour-platings of ice, and every slope was deep in snow. The day which had begun on the moor at a leisurely autumnal pace was suddenly confronted with rock-solid ice-cold deep midwinter. The transition had taken two dawdling hours, including a coffee break.

We assessed the slopes, discussed a leisurely walk back down the corrie instead (we had strapped on ice axes as an afterthought back at the car and discounted the need for crampons – not smart), and lured on by the yellow sunlight rimming the corrie's cornices we kicked into the slope and climbed. Within minutes I was cutting steps and growing mildly alarmed at the prospect of the next almost vertical slope which barred the way to easier ramps above. Even Cameron, a much more accomplished climber, was giving some thought to his surroundings. I made a polite inquiry, the implication of which was a considered retreat, and was relieved that it met with agreement. We gingered back down our cut steps, traversed to a wide shelf, drank more coffee, took stock. We were both suddenly grinning hugely, relishing every step, every movement, every judgment, joyous in our surroundings – the Being again.

We found a kinder slope and cut and kicked our way up and out of Coire Garbhlach, on to another long slow slope whose horizons widened and widened, whose winter deepened and deepened, whose last vague gesture underpinned one more of Nan Shepherd's telling observations: 'This is not done easily nor in an hour . . . However often I walk on them, these hills hold astonishment for me. There is no getting accustomed to them.'

Now there was one more astonishment, for it is reasonable in other landscapes to climb such a corrie and emerge to some kind of summit, a signalling of achievement, a badge of recognition for endeavour, the mountain's small acknowledgment. Here is no such thing.

You emerge from Coire Garbhlach to find yourself nowhere. Oh, there are points of reference – Cairn Toul and Braeriach shapelessly draped across the eastern skyline, the Monadhliaths ranged down the western flank of Strathspey, the scoops and prows of Sgoran Dubh above the trough of Gleann Einich – but between any of these and your stance on the rim of the corrie there is just the rolling, dipping, flattening, climbing, sprawling dimensions of Am Moine Mhor, the Great Moss. You have not climbed to a summit at all, but to a space.

The snow here has been flailed by the wind into impacted wavelets, the grass bloated by ice so that every erect blade is perhaps ten times its own thickness, a small shimmering ankle-high forest with no end, no beginning, no shape, no form, only a space. Yet such is the topography of the Cairngorms, such the repertoire of its myriad corries, that if you could walk from the top of Coire Garbhlach at precisely the same altitude across a flat plain to Braeriach you would find yourself three hundred feet below the *bottom* of Coire an Lochain. You cannot, of course, for the Great Moss roller-coasters subtly through contours of its own, masking them with its space and with a sky which intimidates by rendering even this landscape puny. Even when you climb to the summit cairn of Ben Mac Dhui, there is no sense in which you have reached the top of anything. The focal point mountains are all elsewhere, arranged round distant skylines . . . say the Knoydart peaks or Ben Nevis or Schiehallion. Yet from any one of these far peaks, it is not any one of the Cairngorms which stands out, but a single mass. From the heart of the Cairngorms or half a nation away, that single truth re-emerges again and again – not a mountain range but a singular matchless mountain.

More snow buntings bowled across the plateau, pausing to feed in the lee of a small drift, rising again to explore the wind's bidding. Up here, only people and eagles – and briefly, ptarmigan – contemplate journeyings into the face of the winter wind.

I stood a long time on that unidentifiable spot, apparently fussing over camera lenses, in reality permitting my eyes to wander through and over the shades of blue and white and grey and gold. The winter plateau has rarely time for any other shades, but the trickeries it achieves with these four, the spells it weaves with its winds, are a palette rich enough for any colourist. I tried, too, to assemble the thoughts and sensations crammed into the Cairngorms microcosm which we had just negotiated. All are familiar experiences to the hardened Cairngorms wanderer, but within that familiarity there is a perpetual variety. I threw another phrase of Nan Shepherd's back at Cameron as we returned to Glen Feshie and the autumn we had left behind hours before: 'The thing to be known grows with the knowing.'

The only disappointment about Coire Garbhlach is its name, for it translates as nothing more intriguing than 'the Corrie of the Rugged Country'. Given the intensely poetic nature of the Gaelic language, you fall to wondering about the subtleties of place names which have succumbed to the indifference and incompetence of the cartographers and translators of the centuries. Is it really reasonable to conclude that the tribe who conferred 'An t-Amadan Mointeach' (the fool of the peat moss) on the dotterel, and who could identify a small rickle of stones as 'Ruigh Bristidh Cridhe' (the shieling of the broken heart), would devise nothing better than 'rugged country' for such a phenomenon as Coire Garbhlach?

Even less likely is the Garbh Coire of Braeriach – 'The Rugged Corrie' is almost fatuous in its ruthless logic – and Loch Coire an Lochain emerges merely as 'the loch of the corrie of the lochan'. It is hard to believe that the Gaels of yore did not do much better than these, but the language hereabouts has become a museum piece, a reference work, sustained only by a handful of unquenchable enthusiasts. The landscape suffers because it speaks to us in that tongue to which most of us are deaf. Our understanding of it is impoverished, and therefore we too suffer. It is a two-edged sword, the death throes of a language.

The Garbh Coire is not so much rugged as raw, not so much a corrie as a gargantuan yawn of the mountain's jaws, a vast breach in the west wall of the Lairig Ghru, a thing of such dimensions, such limitless scope, that it accommodates its own corries in its walls. Coire Garbhlach is a portal of the mountain's western periphery, an entrance and an exit of the mountain kingdom; the Garbh Coire is an affair of the heartland, a long day's march in and out of its recesses in any direction. It is, of all the Cairngorms' arenas, the one where I have been least comfortable to be alone.

I climbed on a placid monochrome day up out of Speyside, up out of the Lairig Ghru, to find the mountain's chill bearing down on me out of the Garbh Coire like a waterfall. The corrie itself was furiously grey, the wind stirring and shifting its swirled cloud storms, the ptarmigan huddled low and setting down again almost as soon as they had taken to flight, a reluctant alarm. The new-born Dee, which in less careworn seasons than this back-end of winter capers strenuously down from its plateau womb over the rim of the Garbh Coire Daith (simply 'the rugged corrie of the Dee'; an upper chamber of the Garbh Coire proper), now iced coyly over the precipice in a hung curtain of greenish-white. Somewhere impenetrably deep within these imprisoned Falls of Dee a trickle of the river still flowed, emerging below the falls to wheel headily down into the murky oblivion of the Lairig Ghru.

The immobilised fall is a place to pore over the upheavals and agonies of the birth of the river, a river nursed into life in a cradle mad with the shouted lullabies of the winter wilderness. I sat by the fall and tried to piece together every stretch of the Dee I could think of, every milestone from eagle-scoured Bod an Deamhain – Devil's Point – to the douce, eider-cruised emergence into the sea at Aberdeen more than eighty miles away.

Then I tried to retrace the journey upstream, the river darkening as my mind's journey moved west again, past the river's first glimpse of mighty Lochnagar, its sudden lurch into the mountain landscape of Ben A'an and Beinn a Bhuird, the roughening of its edge as it swerves beyond the Linn of Dee into Glen Dee to be baulked again by Bod an Deamhain where that mountain pyramid presides over its Cairngorms crossroads. I had been telling myself I knew this place, this corrie, this water, that glen, these mountain shapes. But now I thought of all the days, and especially all the winter mountain nights, when the river poured on without pause, minutely reshaping the land as it ploughed its singular furrow down through the mountain's granite heart . . . all these days and nights when I was not here to watch it. The life and energy which brushed by and spattered my boots in the Garbh Coire is a force I find quite beyond comprehension, a thing to marvel at, but in its own way a thing of cheerlessness too for the way in which it crushes to flimsy inconsequentialities the life's achievement of a solitary man. Yet nature at its winter games can take even the river's life and stifle it with the all-consuming forces of ice. In that Ice-Age-fashioned arena, with the iced fall for company, a fragment of Robert Frost's poetry lodged in a corner of my mind:

> Some say the world will end in fire,
> Some say in ice.

From what I've tasted of desire
   I hold with those who favour fire,
But if I had to perish twice,
   I think I know enough of hate
To say that for destruction ice
   Is also great
And would suffice.

Here and alone, I felt a new appreciation of the sentiment.

Two weeks later, I was on my way to the Garbh Coire again, this time from Deeside, on a showpiece winter day and in company. Fred Gordon is another of that small band of individuals I can number on one hand with whom I will cheerfully share a day in such mountainous company. He has run his own mountain holiday business, Grampian Wild Land Guides, he is a superb guide and interpreter of the landscape, a deep thinker and persuasive lecturer on almost every aspect of wild land, an accomplished botanist and biologist, and as rooted in the soil of his native Aberdeenshire as a Scots pine or a granite boulder. He is as addictively thirled to the Cairngorms of Deeside as Cameron McNeish is to those of Speyside. This curious Cairngorms dichotomy persists among their addicts, whose common ground and cementing bond is that ultimate glacial spoor of the Scottish Highlands, the Lairig Ghru.

Expeditionary objectives in Fred's company have often proved to be notional, often derailed by our mutual enthusiasm for diversion and detail and wildlife and tea, not necessarily in that order. So I had set the notional objective of the Garbh Coire by way of Glen Luibeg, boarding the Dee in the Lairig Ghru, retracing the river's agonised infancy which had so preoccupied me two weeks before.

We had already been mightily diverted by the time we rounded the shoulder of Carn a Mhaim into the Lairig itself. Down in Glen Luibeg, the Nature Conservancy Council had enclosed two small areas of pinewood in seemingly terminal decline – that old familiar theme of dying trees and murderous quotas of red deer. Beyond the enclosure, the young trees grow no higher than the tops of the heather before the onslaught begins. A twenty-year-old tree will be a foot high and going nowhere. Inside the enclosure, where the deer are excluded, the trees prosper thickly, the undergrowth burgeons, and having been given that small helping hand nature leaps enthusiastically to its own defence. It is a small and wonderfully eloquent assembly of irrefutable evidence. Its symbolic potential to begin to do something like justice to this perpetually cheated landscape is immense. But its tiny scale was all the NCC had been able to negotiate with the landowner.

By one of these enclosures we pondered the difficulties in the way of progress with Dick Balharry, the NCC's chief warden in north-east Scotland, a chance encounter of old acquaintances, hill fellows well met. Dick is both a visionary and a practical man of action and this was his way of beginning to do what must be done, giving nature a kick-start as he put it.

Such work can go on while the bigger issues of land use and abuse increasingly throng the political agendas, where they must ultimately be resolved. All around the Cairngorms it is noticeable that the only plantations of any size which are fenced off are commercial ones, almost all of them sitka spruce. The sitkas have an economic value, the pines do not, other than a meagre and dwindling shelter for deer, and of course food for deer. A curse is what it is, but there is no point in cursing the deer. The blame lies in the landowners' blind eyes and self-interest and politicians' uninterest, and in the failure of both even to attempt to grasp the significance of landscape for its own sake.

The Glen Luibeg enclosures, however, are a beginning, and they echo a much more ruthless assault by the NCC on the red deer of Creag Meagaidh on Loch Lagganside. There a dying birchwood has been startlingly resurrected, and the whole mountainside plant community, from lochside to summit, utterly transformed. By 1985, Creag Meagaidh had seemed doomed to the lowest common denomination of plantation forestry, having been bought by a private forestry company. Conservationist protest raged, and in the midst of the furore the NCC plotted a daring course founded on a series of drastic measures. First they bought the mountain from the forestry company, so highly did they value its significance as a perfect mirror of landscape change since the Ice Age. Desperate measures have attended their efforts ever since, a sustained, innovative and revolutionary campaign. Its aim is to turn back tides of dereliction, legacy of the deer forest regime, which, compounded by sheep, had brought the mountain wildlife to its knees and the birchwood to the edge of extinction.

It was a stark choice. Either the deer and the sheep go, or the birchwood goes. The sheep went at once and the deer have been going ever since, either being trapped and sold live to deer farms or shot – a policy of land management which has baffled and infuriated landowning traditionalists because it accords priority to the landscape and denies the role of red deer as sacred cow.

The point is cunningly made to visitors. As you walk between two fields to reach the open hill, you are invited to consider the field on the right with its enclosed herd of browsing deer and its shorn grass, then the field on the left with its flourishing birch, alder, rowan, juniper, tall grasses and flowers. The difference is the deer.

Still the neighbouring landowners talk about 'culling' their own deer and the NCC 'slaughtering' theirs, but Dick Balharry explained the NCC position thus: 'It is not deer we count here, but birches. Once we reach a level of regeneration at which the forest can hold its own, we will know the deer population which the mountain can maintain.'

It is nothing less than a revolution. It demonstrates how drastic are the solutions which must be brought to bear if the Cairngorms are to win back their true wilderness.

The day which Fred and I had chosen for the Garbh Coire expedition was simply the best which winter can muster. It had snowed to about 1,500 feet and frozen; the sky bore no cloud and almost no wind, and ranged through every shade of blue from almost white to almost navy; every mountain edge shone; cornices unfurled glitter-rimmed like breaking surf. Glen Geusachan wore a glacier-blue sheen, its walls as hard and smooth as a polished granite tomb. Tomb it is, too, for it means 'Glen of the Pines' but there is no longer a living tree throughout its length. It enshrines silent white stumps, however, bleached headstones to their own green yestreens. From high on Carn a Mhaim, its desolate crescent reinforces the value of what has begun in the pinewood enclosures of Luibeg.

We eased across the mountain's hard snow gullies, climbed to where the snow lay more easily on a long terrace high above the floor of the Lairig and the air was an exhilarating icy rasp in our throats. Fox and hare tracks scoured the place, and ptarmigan scrolled yards of reversed arrowheads. The small dash of stoat was legible too. Then we came to the prints which stopped *us* in our tracks.

Almost in unison we diagnosed, 'Christ, otter!' Five webbed and clawed 'fingers' and the occasional shallow furrow of the tail in softer snow were proof enough, and we lost and found that trail over half a mile of mountainside, all of it well above two thousand feet. We clutched at straws of explanation – an animal crossing from Spey to Dee but shunning the lower man-scent of the footpath? in search of play on the huge gully slides, or in search of grouse or other heather dwellers as prey in days of fish famine?

The late David Stephen wrote that 'Although highly specialised for his life in the water, the otter has not become an over-specialised hunter. He can become a land-weasel when he has to, or wants to . . . ' I knew David Stephen a little and loved his work a lot. He was a blunt, eloquent naturalist who wore his Scottishness like a badge and crusaded for Scotland's wildlife through a clutch of books and thirty years as a newspaper columnist. He once wrote: 'The most dangerous, destructive, wasteful, irresponsible and unteachable animal on earth is the one we see when we view our collective kissers in a keekin glass . . . ' which is as appropriate to the dereliction of the Cairngorms wilderness as any sentence I can think of.

Fred Gordon and I sunned ourselves in the midst of the land-weasel's signatures, admiring the corries of Cairn Toul and the drastic sweep of mountainside up into the Garbh Coire itself. Coire Bhro-chan, one of those small satellite corries lodged high in the gods of the Garbh Coire's auditorium, emerged from beyond the flank of Cairn Toul. It means the 'corrie of the porridge', another Gaelic mystery, but on such a day it wore the air more of a saucer of milk than a porridge pan.

We called a halt, eyed the deepening shadows, calculated our return against the hours of daylight and settled for what the day had achieved. We had not confronted the inner sanctum of the Garbh Coire, but we had rekindled our enthusiasm for its setting (we have both known the place in more than one season), and relished with

22   Towards Cairn Toul from the high sprawl of the Moine Mhor – the Great Moss

23   Storm over Loch Einich

24 Braeriach in sunshine, Gleann Einich in shadow

25 Hard times for a red deer stag in midwinter

26 A last view south into Gleann Einich

27 Scattered pines – the edge of the great Caledonian pine forest of Rothiemurchus

28   The Tree of the Return,
       Gleann Einich

every step the wild perfection of the heart of the Cairngorms at its breathtaking best. We had responded to two enlightening diversions and won a deeper regard for the company of a kindred spirit in the wilds.

We sat on through that mesmerising afternoon, using the stove's recalcitrance in the high frosted air as our excuse to dally until it had produced water hot enough for a brew. It would clearly take some time. I prodded Fred into a regurgitation of some of his mountain rescue team exploits, a fraught arena of human endeavour in which the thinnest of lines divides the funny, the farcical and the fatal. The rescuers *must* survive, to which end they lace mountaineering and medical skills and instinctive compassion with a cynical humour which sometimes borders on the sadistic. On that harrowing emotional tightrope they tread – it helps.

First there were the hitch-hikers.

'Two young lads coming through the Lairig Ghru [so often the centre-stage of Cairngorms rescues] got hopelessly lost and were posted missing. Eventually we found them, and it turned out they were on a hitch-hiking holiday. Someone at a youth hostel suggested they should walk through the Lairig, pointed them in the right direction, and they were supposed to turn up at the other end. They didn't of course.

'Because they were hitching from place to place, they had been using a Shell road map of Britain, which was fine for getting from, say, Birmingham to Glasgow and Glasgow to Aviemore. But to walk through the heart of the Cairngorms, they were using the same map. When we asked to see it, there was a single red triangle which said "The Cairngorms" and that was all! Not only were they hopelessly out of their depth in terms of navigation, they had nothing which was remotely suitable to navigate with. Oh, and they were carrying several pints of milk and a stone of tatties . . . which again would have been fine for hitching, but for the Cairngorms . . . ?'

Then there was the memorial service.

'A young lad called Edward had died, far from the Cairngorms which he had loved all his life. We were asked to accompany his father and a minister to scatter his ashes high in the mountains, a perfectly reasonable request.

'At some point the night before, someone had asked where the ashes were, and there were long looks exchanged when he was directed to a Saxa salt tin which had been on the bothy table all weekend.

'Anyway, the following day, we climbed to the chosen spot, the minister said a few words, and the team leader was asked to scatter the ashes. It was flat calm, but the moment he opened the tin one of those freak gusts of wind blew up, and we were all standing there in a semi-circle, covered in Edward.

'We dusted ourselves down desperately suppressing the urge to burst out laughing, but if one of us had started, that would have ruined everything. We composed ourselves with a studied casualness and walked down. The boy's father was well contented with the ceremony.'

Much later, the pub walls rang and rang with mirth.

Then there was the man from the Ordnance Survey . . .

'We were called out to a climber who had broken an ankle up near the mouth of the Garbh Coire. We found him and pitched a tent over him to keep the elements off. It was a nasty day. We bandaged him up, and as we waited for a helicopter we chatted to him to keep his mind off what was obviously a very painful injury. We were surprised to find he worked for the Ordnance Survey. Then we asked where he was going when the accident happened. He jerked a thumb up towards Braeriach and said: 'I was heading for Bennachie there.' It's the kind of thing which makes you wonder about some of their maps!' (Bennachie is a lowly hill on Donside some forty miles to the east . . .)

'One of the classics was a family of ma, pa, son and daughter who went into the tourist information centre in Aviemore and asked for a decent walk for the four of them for the day. They were directed to a walk round Loch Morlich. So they set off on a superb day and ended up at Derry Lodge. [Loch Morlich's terrain is flat and forested and lies below the western fringes of the Cairngorms. Derry Lodge is twenty miles away on the other side of the Cairngorms, and to get there you have to walk right through the Lairig Ghru, the wildest mountain pass in the land which climbs to almost three thousand feet.] At that point we met them, and you can imagine the looks which passed between us when they asked us how to get back to Aviemore.

'"How did you get through the Lairig?"

'"Oh, we just kept on walking because the scenery was so good."
'"But what about Loch Morlich?"
'"Oh, we thought this was a much better walk than Loch Morlich!"
'All they had had with them was a Mars Bar and a sandwich and a small drink of juice each. We ended up driving them to Ballater and having a whip round to give them enough money to take a taxi back to Aviemore, a drive of more than fifty miles.'

If they had not met the rescue team, they would have been twenty miles from their intended destination, going the wrong way, and a couple of hours from darkness. The consequences don't bear thinking about, because sooner or later the consequences turn up, as they did in 1989.

A German tourist took his children aged eight and eleven through the Lairig, intending to be met by his wife at Coylumbridge. When they failed to show up, she raised the alarm, but only after the search had been underway for some time did she mention the fact that he had planned to cross 'high ground'. It was when the search was extended on to Ben Mac Dhui that they eventually met the man descending the mountain alone. When they found the children, the eight-year-old girl was dead and the boy suffering from exposure. Fred was not involved in the rescue, but interpreted thus:

'It was noticeable that there was no response at all from the rescue teams and the police that night [the newspaper reports carried only the terse mountain rescue team comment that conditions were "wintry" – it was August]. They would have been seething with anger, and nothing they might have said would have been printable. That man paid the ultimate price, but I think he deserved to.' This seasoned rescuer bit his own tongue at that for a short, dark silence, then went on in a more considered vein:

'That incident is one example of the scale of the Cairngorms, or the lack of appreciation of the scale, and of how it deceives. If you want to get to Ben Mac Dhui as that guy did, you've got to walk at least six miles before you are at the base of the mountain. Assuming you want to come out again on the same day, you're talking about a twelve-mile walk in addition to the three thousand feet of actual climbing to get to the top of the mountain. Children of that age have no resilience for that kind of journey over that kind of ground.

131

'More than once in the mountain rescue team we ended up with kids in our charge because the adults had no appreciation of where they were taking them.

'Just recently I was out with a small group and we met a party of boys from London going through the Lairig. There were sixty of them – *sixty!* – and their four leaders were all at the back. The boys had almost certainly never climbed a hill before, but someone thought it was a good idea to take them through the Lairig. Some of the boys at the front had seen us cross the burn, and followed us, because at that point it can look like the way the Lairig runs. But we were going somewhere else, and when we stopped to ask them where they were going, we had to redirect them back across the burn.

'They were aghast to learn that they still had fifteen miles to go. They had only done six or seven, and one of them was already exhausted.

'You have to wonder about the quality of the leadership. There is a point when, especially in misty conditions, the "main road" in the Lairig looks as though it runs up into the Garbh Coire. With the leaders all at the back, if some of the kids had gone that way, when were they going to find out about it? – when they got to the other side and found out that ten kids were missing?

'Whenever I go out with groups, and even though they are ninety-nine per cent adults, I'm mentally going "one . . . two . . . three . . . four . . . " every so often just to make sure that someone hasn't gone behind a boulder for a pee.'

Our conversation dwelt on the question of the daunting and deceptive nature of the landscape scale. It is easy enough from a perspective such as Fred Gordon's back-of-the-hand familiarity to see how the Cairngorms might fool walkers and climbers raised on lesser landscapes, even more tightly-packed ones like the Lake District or Glencoe. The extra miles north, the extra thousand feet in height, the tundra nature of the plateau with often no focal point even in good visibility, the invisible treacheries of the winds which kill by chilling . . . all these have no comparable points of reference anywhere in Britain, and the only way to acclimatise to the Cairngorms psychology is to become accustomed to it. There is no shortcut. Fred encapsulated the problem of scale thus:

'Years ago, a Swiss mountain guide came to Edinburgh and was asked how long he thought it would take to get to the top of Arthur's Seat. "Two days," was the reply, at which point he was thrown into a car and driven there in ten minutes. People apply one scale they are familiar with and superimpose it on something else and they can get it totally wrong. In this case, the Swiss guide had converted an eight-hundred-foot hill a mile away into an Alpine peak many miles away because of an impression of size and shape.'

Those fundamental dangers inherent in a lack of appreciation of scale are compounded by the most common failing among those who venture into the Cairngorms – inadequate footwear.

'You see everything from trainers to high-heeled dress shoes, but even lightweight boots give you no ankle support, and are disastrous in the boulderfields. If you fall on a kerb in a city street and break your ankle, you can be in hospital in ten minutes. But if you break your ankle on, say, Derry Cairngorm . . .

'The nearest telephone is four or five miles away at Derry Lodge. By the time your pal, who will probably be suffering from shock and in a panicked state, can get there, it could be two and a half hours. Remember he has got to consider his own safety across the boulder-fields as well. What if that phone is not working? (It's just a public telephone on the wall of a derelict shooting lodge and exposed to all the Cairngorms elements.) He has a five-mile walk to the next phone. But suppose the phone does work. By the time the police alert the mountain rescue team, by the time they muster, drive to Derry Lodge, walk to Derry Cairngorm, find you, we're talking seven hours if you are really lucky and the weather is reasonable. You could have a helicopter at your side much sooner, if everything goes your way – say four hours, minimum. If you're lying there with a broken leg for four hours on your own in the Cairngorms, it's a hell of a long time.'

The implication of all this is that if you are less than lucky, and it's winter, and night falls, and visibility is awful, a helicopter is unlikely to be of much assistance where you're going. It is worth cultivating a healthy respect for the Cairngorms landscape, and buying a decent pair of boots.

Winter slipped inexorably, indistinguishably into April. It does not do to be deceived by bright briskly-breezed mornings on the floor of the glen, the first tree pipits sliding down chutes of song into the crowns of pine and birch, or the grey wagtails' nest in the bank well quilted with gull feathers. These are simply rituals of the passing of the year, and not to be interpreted in the Cairngorms as the passing of winter. April could be its last month, or its second last, or its third last. The weather forecast warned of big winds and snow by the end of the day.

I was high on the Beanaidh Bheag, one of the most delectable of all the Cairngorms mountain burns, chewing contentedly on mushy banana rolls, swilling sweet burn water, scanning the sky for eagles (finding none), throwing eager glances up at Coire an Lochain, the most westerly of a handsome trilogy of corries set deep into the northward prow of Braeriach. The 'lochain' in question lies at 3,300 feet, the highest loch in the land, a place of late spring icebergs and profound depths of water. If I was to pinpoint an abode for my mountain gods, I might choose Coire an Lochain, but these are dangerous trains of thought to explore and best left undisturbed, while you climb at least. Make your peace with the mountain when it offers its hand, not when you feel like offering your own.

I began to fret about the wind the moment I climbed from a small heathery gully into the high open moor. It was a hammering easterly which had seemed innocuous enough in the glen, an old trick in the Cairngorms. You learn to prepare for the trickery but you never learn not to be taken by surprise at the skill and the scale of the deception. By the time I had reached the steep boulderfield which smothers the high slopes of Braeriach, the wind had developed a frightening chill and a gusting ferocity. I was suddenly thrust sideways and propelled towards frozen snow slopes at a quite uncontrolled involuntary run. The nearest snow slope went a long way down. I fell, deliberately, a yard short of it, and lay there while the banshee blew over. I hauled into the lee of a large rock and considered my position. I was alone, unforgivably without an ice axe (although without the wind it would have been simple enough to avoid the snow slopes), but otherwise well equipped. The wind would only worsen as I climbed, and the brightness of the sky was no reassurance against the arrival of snow at any time. I had more than enough daylight, I was fit, I knew the ground, and the prospect of dodgem car icebergs and waterspouts making a mad jig of the loch would be a new taste of the wilderness to savour. I put on every shred of wind-blunting clothing I carried and climbed on. In the next three hundred feet of mountainside, I was blown over at least a dozen times.

On what may well have been the thirteenth occasion, I was bludgeoned far to the right at a frantic pace and caught the edge of a snow slope as I fell. The waterproof trousers which I had just put on to rebuff the wind now eased my passage down the snow with some spectacle. The illusion of slow-motion which attends such moments of crisis allowed me to dwell interminably on how to avoid breaking anything more valuable than a leg; I began to wrestle with the idea of manoeuvring into a sitting position, then slowly effected the manoeuvre so that I was able to bring my heels to bear on the frozen snow. They bit in just enough to allow me to run at a sprinting crouch off the bottom of the slope and slow my momentum before I collided inevitably and unceremoniously with a boulder. I had slid about two hundred feet, and emerged merely breathless. I sat and sheltered for quarter of an hour doggedly keeping at bay a rogue train of thought about the folly of trying to breach the stronghold of the mountain gods.

One way to combat such perverse psychology is with positive physical endeavour. I climbed again, skirting the biggest snow slopes to the west so that I should be blown away from them. I fell again and again, sat down at every gust I could beat to the punch, until at last the ground fell before me, and I was gingering down into the corrie itself, peering through stinging gustfuls of blown iced snow for the spectacle of the loch. There was none.

I sat down again, dumbfounded this time. No loch?

Not the wrong corrie?

I reassured myself . . . three corries, and this the third one.

A white wall climbed impenetrably upwards to where threshing clouds occasionally unveiled a black buttress and sank mysteriously downwards to a smooth and dazzling white corrie floor. This bowl of brilliant light was what had deceived. As the eyes accustomed to its glare I found a darker white stain and a network of awesome cracks, inches wide, feet deep. Then the sun began to spill out, first for moments, then for minutes at a time, so that the light in the corrie flashed and coloured and blued and greyed and revolved as though it was playing off one of those 1950s ballroom globes. I was in the right corrie, and I had my spectacle, but it was not a thing of waterspouts and icebergs because the loch was under six feet of ice and frozen snow. The dark white stain showed where the snow had almost blown clear of the ice.

Down on the corrie floor, the whole mountain world is shut out. There is no view other than the headwall and the tumult of skies. Only the wind found a way in. It beat about the corrie with undiminished fervour, but it could not unhinge the sense of sanctuary which inhabits these walls.

Three things surprised me about Coire an Lochain. I had only seen it before from above and in summer when its waters wore that milky greenish clarity associated with glacial waters the Arctic world over. The first was that having climbed to its lowest lip it should be necessary to climb *down* into the corrie. The second was the sheer size of it – not on a scale comparable with the Garbh Coire, but somehow I expected that the highest loch in Britain should also be the tiniest, and peering down from a thousand feet above had not disillusioned me. But it is a big loch to be kept so furtively secure from the prying eyes of every inch of the Cairngorms bar Braeriach's summit plateau. The third surprise was the raw, silent desolation which the wind did not broach for all its roar. There are deeper silences in the wildest landscapes which go beyond surface things. You hear one sometimes on a May moorland when a stanza of curlew song ends or the falling note of golden plover dips into its oblivion and there is a gap, ocean-deep, of seconds, before any other sound can register. Today in Coire an Lochain, I had been deafened by the wind's incessant bruising for hours, and had won an immunity, if not from its force, at least from its loud wrath. The thousand-foot snow wall's uncompromising glare, a sheet hung from the mountain's summit, was the guardian of a formidable silence.

Something glittered on a blasted heather stem, a brilliant white, crazily dancing thing, right on the lip of the corrie where the wind did its worst. It was a ptarmigan feather, ensnared by the Arctic stubbornness of the bird's tribe and the unquenchable thirst for life of the plant under this most brutal of regimes. The wind which could lift my thirteen stones bodily from a boulder was beaten by a feather. I crouched between the feather and the wind, cupped mitted hands round it, and still failed to slow its dizzy dance, but ten minutes later, when I stood to go, heather and feather were still wedded. That too provided humiliations of a kind for a mere mortal.

I disturbed two ptarmigan on the same slope, tholing the wind with the immunity which is their inherited privilege in this their kingdom. They flew fifty yards, low upwind, then began to walk back across the snow to the rocks where they had first risen. The male was already darkening about the flanks and cock-tailed; the female, still white, tail low, led the uncanny procession. The two birds, the amputated feather, the wind-flocked snow crystals, the mad mountain air and I were all that stirred there.

I contemplated my descent, skidding before the wind across the highest boulders, wondering (with a hint of revenge for a secondary motive) how I might make use of a long narrow snow slope, how to effect a long glissade without an ice axe with which to steer and brake. I scoured a patch of scree and found two fist-sized stones roughly axe-head shaped, and, after a trial run on a short diagonal course, set off at the same blistering speed which characterised my first involuntary snow slide. Now with the stones in each hand I could steer and brake, and I whooped down eight hundred feet in what seemed like seconds. I stood up at the bottom and looked back. Coire an Lochain had already withdrawn remarkably, and of the Loch of the Corrie of the Lochan itself there was no hint. I boarded a second snow slope, hurtled two hundred feet more, and found myself beyond the boulders, beyond the roar of the wind.

In that instant of the silenced banshee, that great headlong eagle flight I had watched cross my pinewood horizon five winter months ago lurched vividly into mind. What had I endured compared to what the eagle had? Was there any common ground at all in the sensation I now felt – a blissful release – and that which the eagle would know when he finally furled his wings on some sheltered crag of his journey's end, the winter winds finally stilled from about his head?

As I dawdled down the Beanaidh Bheag into the glen, I felt an elation which was rooted not in any sense of physical accomplishment, for that will always be at the mountain's whim, but in my share of the day's landscape. In the winter of 1987 I had helped to edit a publication for the Scottish Wild Land Group called *Cairngorms at the Crossroads*. Among its contributors was the doyen of all Scottish mountaineering writers, W.H. Murray, and among his sentiments were these, which I now recalled: 'Cairngorms days bring endless surprise: fear, exhilaration, suspense, idyllic ease – you can never tell what will be next, save that here is living.'

Deep in the glen I paused by the edge of the pinewoods and, because it seemed it was being offered, made my peace with the mountain.

> The calendar rewound
> (spring into winter) as I climbed
> between Gleann Einich and Braeriach's
> brutal boulderfield. Winds
> born in dire December
> frittered away my April where
> the contours crammed closer.
> Snow buntings flew compulsorily west
> above the couched and contemplative deer
> while suns blinked and blinked
> amid the debris of shredding cumulus.
>
> Only I, it seemed, of all
> Braeriach's moving morsels, fought
> the wind (climbing's every battle's
> waged against the grain), floundering,
> falling, finally felled.
> I heard caution's silent counsel then
> balance that sage 'beware' against
> the mountain's siren song
> whose lilt friends have died for.
> Who am I to turn deaf ears now?
>
> I climbed again to win
> Braeriach's blue-veined heart

        where winds part only to permit
        a ptarmigan's safe passage. I thanked
        the mountain's winter god then slid away
        down the months-long snows
        to April in the glen.

But the long winter of the high corries which rivets lochans to rock floors with ice for seven or eight months at a time slowly relents, suddenly unlocks a miser's hoard of alpine flowers for a few weeks of July or August. It is an opportunist tribe of plants which emerges in the lee of the old snows, seizing fragments of succour in the unlikeliest places, prising lifeblood from landscapes where soil is as thin on the ground as windless days.

A few dare the thin soil and fat winds of the plateau itself, brief glories passing across the face of the mountain like the ghost of a smile. In the poorest of summers you can climb here every week but two and miss the whole show. In the case of the rare curved woodrush, it's the ghost of a ghost of a smile, for few plants own up to less conspicuous flowers than these dull green clusters. Guidebooks are fond of the phrase 'nodding clusters' for the curved woodrush flowerheads, which suggests an unfamiliarity with the plateau winds. If you find them at all, they are more likely to be bowed compliantly before the blast, the nodding clusters bouncing berserkly on the end of impossibly flimsy spindles of plants.

It is that apparent impossibility of the evidence of your eyes which characterises the flowers of the high Cairngorms. Here is thrift, 'sea pinks' of everyone's favourite seaside, a pink shock of flowers as wide as a carpet, or at least a decent hearth rug, at four thousand feet. Why should it thrive at sea level and at the summit of the land, but nowhere in between? And what persuades a common dog violet to lodge here, confounding the guidebooks ('March to June, sea-level to 1,000 feet') by flowering in August at four thousand feet?

Alpine lady's mantle flowers are outshone by their leaves, handsome fat stars of dark green, wondrously silvered beneath, with the vigour to grow thick as matting in places. The flowers, a barely visible pale yellowish green, do not add to the plant's appeal even in full bloom. Its Latin name of *Alchemilla alpina* indicates a plant which found favour with the alchemists of yore for its healing powers, and indeed it was used particularly for what people of a certain age call 'women's problems'. Not least of its properties is a reputation for uplifting bosoms which have slumped past their prime, but whether the leaves should be applied externally or taken internally has not been handed down. There is also no known connection, or even a fanciful theory I can devise, between such properties and the fact that lady's mantle is named after the Virgin Mary.

Saxifrages creep across the corries too, from the bold purple saxifrage (flowers massed as thick as bees on a comb) to the discreet yellow mountain saxifrage and the collector's piece tufted saxifrage. If you stumble on one of these, keep your mouth shut and leave it be, for the predations of collectors have already accounted for the demise of several botanical rarities in the high Cairngorms.

I have an illogical affection for another of the saxifrage tribe which stems perhaps from nothing more than the charming nature of our first acquaintance. I once pulled a sixpence from my pocket with a handkerchief (this was years ago when I habitually carried both). The coin lodged irretrievably in a fissure, but I fingered down around the 3,500-feet contour just in case, and more because I don't like dropping evidence of my passing on mountains than because I was over-whelmed with grief at the loss of a sixpence. I found not silver but gold, the small gold audacity of a starry saxifrage rooted in a tiny black chasm. A fluke of the sun spotlit the single four-inch stem and its three flowerheads but left the walls of its underground chamber unlit and coal black, thrusting the flowers into showpiece focus. Each flower is a perfect five-point white star, every petal tinily daubed with two canary yellow spots and overlaid with bright red anthers. The nature of the find was so intense that it has survived indelibly the intervening years. I have often weighed the deal since then – a sixpence for a saxifrage. No mountain before or since has offered me such value for money.

I left silver and gold where I lost and found them, forging (as I fancied) a new alloy of the mountain. The whole mountain is an alloy, a vast landmass shot through with a million wildlife dramas as blatant as a deer herd or a pair of eagles, as lowly as lichens, as sunny and starry as saxifrages, as taut as a sprig of goldenrod.

Goldenrod has the perfect pedigree for a mountain landscape like the Scottish Highlands, whose bloodier eras were carved and lacerated with broadsword and dirk and *sgian dubh*, and washed down with copious draughts of claret of uncertain vintage. The antidote for such a way of life was goldenrod, for as an ointment it was known to heal wounds, and as a hot drink cured ailments of the liver and kidney, or so the stories go. At any rate its generic Latin name of *Solidago* implies a relationship with the verb *solidare* which means to heal. A small splash of golden yellow flower high on a bouldery flank of a Cairngorms corrie is certainly a sight for sore eyes.

IO

The Spirit of the High and Lonely Places

I HAVE CLIMBED TO THE SUMMIT of the land. It is warm and still and summery. Winter, for a few brief days, perhaps weeks, has abdicated his kingdom. It is early July and it has not snowed here for two weeks now. I sit somewhere between the Wells of Dee and the Einich Cairn of Braeriach, incubating the spirit of this high and lonely land with all the couched determination of a brooding ptarmigan.

My seat is a random choice. There is no wind to deflect, no need for water for a brew (I have slaked my thirst at the Wells an hour ago), no mountain destination in mind other than the one I have reached. I have suddenly lost the urge to walk so I sit, comfortable in my surroundings as any granite boulder. I sit to be closer to the landscape, to be a boulder. By a fluke of contours and sightlines I have no view other than the plateau, no horizon other than the plateau's visual limitations. I am at a little over four thousand feet, and yet I have no view.

The summit of this land is a top floor. Sit in the middle of the top floor of any building anywhere where there are no taller buildings in its surroundings, and all you can see is the floor itself and the sky. So I sit and watch the floor and the sky, and the spirit of the high and lonely places wells to a thumping mountain heartbeat.

What is it, this spirit, which Seton Gordon invoked on the summit of Lurcher's Crag? Remember the form of words?

In the immense silences of these wild corries and dark rocks, the spirit of the high and lonely places revealed herself, so that one felt the serene and benign influence that has from time to time caused men to leave the society of their fellows and live on some remote surf-drenched isle – as St Cuthbert did on Farne – there to steep themselves in those spiritual influences that are hard to receive in the crowded hours of human life . . .

The spirit is, I think, a collaboration of landscape forces, of light, of weather, of space, the mingled chemistry of which creates a tangible presence of nature that demands a response in those who encounter it. Respect for the spirit is the first commandment of the wilderness, and its inviolability should be the first consideration of all those who pronounce on the Cairngorms.

The spirit lingers most blatantly on the plateau. There is no mountain sensation to compare with its sweeping plain, its corner-to-corner skies, the concealed knowledge of its corrie theatres whose dramas are carved into its flanks, the restlessness of its air which can wash great freedoms through a receptive human mind in the manner of St Cuthbert's surf. The spirit tramples the land in its storms, clings to every rock and stem and leaf and berry as the ptarmigan feather clings to the blasted heather stem.

The spirit forages with the eagle, the ptarmigan, the dipper, the otter, the fox, the hare, the wren, the crevice-hunting spider, the teeming pinewood ants, the pines themselves where they dare the wind on Creag Fhiaclach, the small spread of moss and saxifrage, the peat-moss-foolery of the dotterel. The spirit in its unique Cairngorms distillation is Arctic. It is hard, harsh, elemental, unluxurious, the garb of a landscape pared to the bone.

To be alone on the plateau, to sit boulder-still and warm and let your mind range over all the Cairngorms landscapes of half a lifetime and all their weathers, to climb, as it were, through the landscapes of your mind anchored to a belay of unflinching granite, is to know finally the touch of the spirit. Reach down through the years from the summer boulder to dark pinewood winters when the sun slept for a week and high noons were indistinguishable from their dawns and dusks, and recognise the same exalted common denominator, their rootedness in the same mountain embrace, the touch of the same spirit. There is a uniformity of presence which attends every step of your way from Spey to Dee, and it is that uniformity, translated by Seton Gordon as the spirit of the high and lonely places, which so distinguishes and dignifies all the Cairngorms, all their moods, all their heights and depths, all their landscapes.

But if the spirit is unique, it is also fragile. It can only be safeguarded and nurtured by a perpetual and unflinching adherence to the principles of wilderness, a commitment for all time. But it can be undermined and obliterated at a single thoughtless stroke. It is quite extinct between Coylumbridge and the Cairngorm plateau where first forestry, then tourism, then skiing, and now all three, have fashioned a wrecking conspiracy which has inflicted degrading and alien values on the finest mountain prospect in the land, torturing and tarnishing it, possibly for all time. It is true that the conspiracy has won a measure of prosperity and provided new if unreliable jobs (there is no more fickle employer in the Highlands than one which relies on the weather). It has also created at Aviemore one of the least indigenous communities in the Highlands while agencies charged with economic development cluck their approval and demand more of the same. Meanwhile the lifeblood of the golden goose which makes it all possible – the Cairngorms landscape – seeps from the wounds.

The first public overtures in 1989 of the ski developers' revised ambitions for Lurcher's Gully, where Seton Gordon composed his eulogy sixty-four years earlier, were couched in a mood of 'reasonable' *bonhomie*, and heralded by the slogan 'The Cairngorms – Room for All'. The argument for expansion hinged on the statistic that even after development the area of the Cairngorms 'affected by downhill skiing' would amount to under two per cent of the whole, and a tiny coloured blob on a map 'proved' it.

On the ground, however, the area affected by downhill skiing includes everything from Aviemore to the summit of Ben Mac Dhui, every long long view into the wounded corries of Cairngorm for miles up and down Strathspey, every short-sighted manifestation of the fast-food quick-buck culture along miles of roadside, including – in Aviemore – credit card signs nailed to a tree.

The disrespect for landscape is contagious. It only takes one major development to establish the precedent which breaches the sanctity of wilderness. Other developers will always have a head start in the

Cairngorms because the Cairngorm skiing development is there. Children are introduced to the mountain by way of a ski-tow and learn that the corries are valued only as exploitable resources. They are blind to the turned backs of eagles, deaf to the voice from afar of the spirit of the high and lonely places. Thus are sown the seeds of a greater destruction.

But skiing is only the most recent recruit to the forces ranged against the Cairngorms. Slavish adherence to the archaic economics of the deer forest brings death to the pinewoods, particularly in the eastern Cairngorms. Attitudes to land ownership are exemplified by the fact that, while the RSPB, for example, has bought pinewoods in Abernethy on Speyside to save them and encourage their expansion, a succession of landowners on the other side of the Cairngorms pursue policies which have precisely the opposite effect. Yet in a mountain landscape acclaimed internationally *as landscape* there remains no Government policy to stimulate one and inhibit the other. It remains to be seen whether any Cairngorms World Heritage Site fares better than St Kilda has done, whether the Government decides to own up to the responsibilities implicit in World Heritage Site designation, and offer more than lip service.

The deer forest inflicts other injuries on the spirit. The lacerations of bulldozed roads speed Land-Rovers and other estate vehicles far across the plateau. There are thousands of miles of such tracks deep into the mountain heartland accommodating the expensive tastes of shooters who are not prepared to walk. Legislation which sought to limit their worst excesses has been a woeful failure, as great a slight to the landscape for its insipidness as the fact of the tracks is for its brutality. Years of conservation protest have made no impact.

Low-flying aircraft startle the spirit into retreat, helicopters plague it with almost daily regularity, even mere pedestrians belittle it with mass events and noise and litter and garish clothing and equipment. All these and lesser conflicts drive the spirit into the furthest flung recesses of the Cairngorms, to ration its hours of tangibility to a dwindling scarcity. Yet it is only by honouring the spirit, by a return to the simple unimpeachable wisdom of the values upon which it thrives, that the landscape can be saved. The osprey, the goldeneye, the realistic hopes of re-establishing the red kite, demonstrate that some of it at least is retrievable, but only if attitudes relent, only if the landscape – the habitat of all wildness – is healed.

The prevailing wisdom among the countryside bureaucrats in Scotland is that the solution lies in a national park system, and the Cairngorms have long represented the Countryside Commission for Scotland's trailblazing national park ideal. It confirmed that with the publication of the 1990 report 'The Mountain Areas of Scotland'. The Cairngorms was one of four suggested national parks, the others being Loch Lomond and the Trossachs, Ben Nevis/Glen Coe/Black Mount, and Wester Ross. The need for a park in the Cairngorms was 'urgent' the report said. The portents, however, are not good, either for the Scot who still follows the landscape tradition into which he was born (and those who journey from beyond Scotland and eagerly share it) or more importantly for the landscape itself. National parks have failed the landscapes of England and Wales by their inability either to embody their original long-lost ideals in enforceable legislation, or to stem the flood of visitor pressure which years of relentless promotion and self-flattery have generated. The degradation of the Lake District is a prospect for the Cairngorms and all Scotland to eye askance. It should be remembered that the World Heritage Site submission for the Lake District was rejected by UNESCO because of such degradation.

Neither the Commission in Scotland or local authorities – the two compulsory foundation stones of any national park structure in the Cairngorms – have endeared themselves to champions of wilderness. Too many councillors see a national park only as Lakeland-style gravy train. The Lakeland experience has shown them that a defiled, exploited landscape is no deterrent to a certain strain of tourism, and all they would have to lose by so exploiting the Cairngorms is their credibility in the international conservation community, already aghast at Scotland's lack of commitment to its best and wildest landscape. The Commission sees in a national park system that which it has always lacked, a credible *raison d'être*. The ideology of a national park would be compromise, a mild variation on the ski developers' 'room for all' theme. Of course there is room for all, but only if we are to preside over the execution of the landscape – death by unnatural causes.

On the plateau, I watched the sky change – attitude, mood, colour, light, and, ultimately, season. A greying cloud swelled and swerved from the west, lured, it seemed, by the spell of the mountain. It reached Braeriach, blackening and furious, flinging fast rains, draining the rock of its sun-fire, cloaking the plateau in an array of chills, peppering it with hailstones. Finally and briefly it snowed, and I added a new month to my snow calendar. The dervish was done in ten minutes and raced on to torment some other boulder dweller, unlocking the sun again and trailing a rainbow behind it. I watched its furious drunken dance stumble down and up the Lairig Ghru, flay Ben Mac Dhui, lurch on down the throat of Cairngorm's blind side, and blot out the mountain entirely.

For a moment there was no Cairngorm, nothing east of the Lairig but a rainbow jiving on a black backcloth. I bathed in my restored summer watching winter's pointed reminder, a guerrilla band unwilling to honour the terms of the ceasefire because the warring of the seasons is much more stimulating than the peace.

The rest of that mountain day shone and tingled with the wake of that small wintry epilogue, or was it an overture? The plight of these mountains had been much on my mind, and I now imagined that storm cloud as a chariot of the spirit of the high and lonely places, a courier of dark tidings, and from its shouts and whispers fashioned a meaning in its rainbow.

The red is the blaze at the fingertip of the tiny cladonia lichens, the flame of the spirit, rooted in granite.

The orange is the eye of the eagle, the vigilance of the wilderness, patrolling the territory of the spirit on 'death's-dark-angel's' wings.

The yellow is the bugling bill of the whooper swan, Arctic anthem of the spirit.

The green is the pinewood, cloak of the spirit, an unbroken lineage ten thousand years back to the Ice.

The blue is the summer watersheet of the osprey loch, rekindling of the spirit, the indigo and violet the autumn and winter dusk skies of the same shore, now loud with the throats of geese and a small, fluctuating and aloof chorus of unmuted whooper trumpets.

Such is my rainbow. I wish my fellow man in this landscape the unquenchable tenacity of the cladonia, the vigilance and the tolerance and the predatory judgment of the eagle, the anthem of the wilderness in his ears, a cloak of hodden green to blunt the storms, and, to root his ambitions for wilderness not in terms of years but millennia, the loyal and lasting flexibility of a single watersheet. I hope he will learn again what he once knew when he lived closer to the land, closer to the animal state, which is to respect rather than resent that nature will always outshine him, the land always outlast him; to acknowledge that there is no pot of gold at the rainbow's end, only a piece of the wilderness which is in better heart than it was simply because the rainbow touched and blessed and danced on.

I watched my rainbow dance on and fade, watched the thwarted summer dash over the plateau again. Slowly the place stilled, grew warm, wore its rarest guise, a basking wilderness. Is there the remotest possibility that we will ever do justice to this of all our landscapes? Will we be forever hell-bent on its merciless exploitation, or will the social historians of a later century look back at this small era in the Cairngorms' long emergence from the Ice and mark it down for a turning point, the shift of a tide from the ebb of indifference to the flow of awareness?

There is only one choice facing the Cairngorms now. Either the mountains become a playground – more profitable, more exploitable, more polluted, less and less wild – or we go back, own up to crimes against the landscape, dismantle the playground, commit ourselves to wilderness and accord nature the upper hand again.

Compromise has given us what we have now, and that satisfies no one other than a handful of bureaucrats who worship at the shrine of consensus because that is the path to knighthoods and other lesser New Year's honours. But for as long as the principle of development within the Cairngorms is countenanced, developers will always want to develop more, for that is the nature of the beast. For as long as conservationists are embattled and embittered by successive rearguard actions seeking to defeat or compromise the next development and the next, defending the landscape will be perceived by many people as a negative stance and a barrier to progress and prosperity. The landscape, meanwhile, is demeaned, locked into a spiral of decline by the perpetual quest for compromise.

Existing legislation is no match for the commercial pressures which well up around the fringes of the Cairngorms, and without stronger legislation it is a question of time before the heartland of the mountains is breached again as massively as it has been on Cairngorm itself. Fred Gordon projected one such all too believable example: 'The state that the Cairngorms are in now, one more bad idea could be disastrous. Who knows when there might come a point that a road up Glen Quoich on to Beinn a Bhuird becomes commercially viable? There is so much clamour for skiing that you could demand as much as you want from skiers to use such a road. The cost of building the road is apparently what has held up a serious proposition being advanced so far, but as road building techniques advance there will come a point when you can do it for a fraction of the cost that you can do it now. Roll out the carpet and there's your road.' (Beinn a Bhuird already has a vile bulldozed road all the way to its summit plateau for deer stalking and the mountain itself clearly offers great skiing potential. With skiing thus established at both ends of the Lairig Ghru, the much vaunted road through the Lairig would become a major step nearer to nightmarish reality.)

'No, I think you have to say . . . Cairngorms – that's it. No more development.'

So the choice is playground or wilderness, one or the other. There is no 'room for all'.

This book sings the landscape's song because I am for the wilderness. I seek no more compromise – no compromise at all, not for the Cairngorms. I believe the conservation movement, if it is to be seen to be positive and if it wishes to effect real progress here, must go for broke.

The only task worth the effort is to draw up the ideal set of circumstances under which the Cairngorms can flourish as wilderness and, with that single purity of purpose, fight to have them implemented. Keep the rearguard actions for lesser landscapes and lesser battlefronts. In the Cairngorms, seize one historic initiative, make the running, and let developers, the uncaring element among landowners, the bureaucrats and all the other enemies of the Cairngorms landscape dance as best they can to a tune with which they are not familiar. The launch of one sustained and supreme effort could prove to be a watershed beyond which the Cairngorms would be safeguarded as wilderness for all time and society would look at its wild landscapes with new and respectful eyes.

Anything less clings to the futile status quo, and has damage limitation as its highest endeavour. The Cairngorms landscape deserves a higher purpose than that. It will be safe only when its protection is enshrined in law, only when legislation makes it unambiguously clear that the Cairngorms are not available for development, not available for poor land management, not available for thoughtless tourist promotion, not negotiable. Until then, the conflict created by compromise will be the principle arena into which energies are channelled; the landscape will continue to deteriorate; conservation will be condemned to the role of protesting villain and the tactic of the rearguard action, and the public perception of a negative force; even development proposals which have been rejected, such as the Lurcher's Gully scheme, can still be amended and resubmitted again and again if necessary, because the developers know that there is nothing in the planning system to stop it, and that sooner or later the opposition will weary as its resources dwindle and the public tires of its protest.

So if the uniqueness of the Cairngorms is to be recognised and justice is to be done to the landscape, I believe it is necessary to look to a different scale of commitment, a different breed of planning legislation, a different ordering of priorities from anything we have ever contemplated. At the heart of the conservation initiative should be a blueprint for change with unshakable principles:

One – a hundred-year Government commitment to the restoration of the Cairngorms wilderness. A hundred years is the figure Adam Watson has used to indicate how long the worst damage would take to heal, but it is an arbitrary number which may prove to be too short. We have no serious Government involvement in the welfare of wild landscape, a fact which is itself a serious charge to lay against any European nation. 'Restoration of wilderness' would imply the dismantling of every man-made artefact in the mountains, all skiing developments, all roads, car parks, buildings, bulldozed roads, even bothies and bridges, allied to a determined programme of restoration on the ground. It also implies relieving the pressure of people on the ground, if not by physical exclusion then certainly by denying people artificially easy forms of access. Cairngorm would quickly begin to recover, for example, if the nearest car park was at Coylumbridge.

Two – the encouragement and restoration of every indigenous habitat and its wildlife. With the rebirth of an encircling native forest for its cornerstone, the scope and scale of reordering our own priorities in the Cairngorms so that they match nature's is awesome. It cannot be done, however, without the most fundamental reappraisal of land use and land ownership. The landscape must never again be treated as currency as it has been all too often for all too long. Heritage cannot be bought and sold – it can only be honoured and defiled. The reappraisal must decide whether there are too few people owning too much land, whether there should be a maximum holding by any individual, whether to exercise positive discrimination among would-be landowners (and surely concluding that the Highlands and Islands Development Board by definition has no place as a landowner here), whether to consider wholesale acquisition by, say, the Nature Conservancy Council, of those estates which are unwilling to change from the deer forest tradition to a system of land use tailored to the needs of the landscape and sustained by a Government programme to fund practical conservation. (There are problems here – if it is seen that land adjudged important enough to be managed for conservation is bought by conservation organisations, it then becomes more and more difficult to argue the case for that land which is *not* owned by conservation interests.)

Three – a planning regime which would take the Cairngorms out of local authority control, which would preclude development in the Cairngorms heartland and establish rigid principles covering development around the fringes of the mountains 'force-field'. Its policies would be shaped by the best of those professional naturalists and scientists whose work has served the Cairngorms landscape well and who alone know the true worth of that landscape. Conservation's principal recourse under existing planning systems is to respond to development proposals as they arise and defend the landscape against them. There is no opportunity for 'un-developing', in which conservation might contemplate a development which is already on the ground and advance the case for its removal in the interests of the landscape.

Four – a serious study of the employment prospects which conservation on a Cairngorms-wide scale would offer. There would obviously be fewer jobs in tourism, and none at all in skiing, around a Cairngorms dedicated to wilderness, but there would be new opportunities to staff the wilderness initiative with locally recruited and trained people, to reach directly into the school curriculum with conservation-based studies and there introduce the possibilities offered by conservation-based careers.

Having prepared its blueprint, the conservation movement must set about advancing the cause of its principles, and for that it must dare the political arena. Conservation and politics are no strangers to each other in many countries all over the world. On the rare occasions when they pull willingly on the same side, as they did in Scots-born conservation pioneer John Muir's renowned friendship with American president Theodore Roosevelt, bureaucratic mountains can be moved in the interest of real ones. There can be few western nations, however, where there is quite such a distant uninterest and ignorance over both the problems confronting Scotland's wildest landscapes and the deeply felt need within Scotland – indeed throughout Britain – to protect them.

But somewhere along the way, and sooner rather than later, the Cairngorms need a Cairngorms Wilderness Act to enshrine those principles of conservation in law, and to win such an Act conservation must fight the political fight. Skiing will not voluntarily vacate the mountain. Deer forest landowners will not voluntarily abandon the economics of sporting estates. Tourism will not voluntarily strike the view across Loch Morlich to the northern corries from its glossy literature. The leisure industry will not voluntarily abandon one of its most lucrative markets. Planning authorities will not voluntarily concede to the planning principles of nature conservation as first priority. Councillors will not voluntarily give away their planning powers.

Fred Gordon is emphatic about the need for a single Government body 'with real teeth' to oversee the planning process: 'You are almost talking about a Cairngorms ombudsman in some respects, a body which can say this planning proposal is not in keeping with the general principles which we have laid down for the Cairngorms therefore it doesn't go through and that's an end of it. Or this planning application is in keeping, so it can go ahead. You have to look at the Cairngorms as a whole, not only the situation as it is now, but also how all these things which have happened in the past and all the decisions we make now will affect pressures on the Cairngorms in the future. Numbers of people have to be limited to a level which the landscape can cope with, but how can you do that until you get this body politic which is responsible for the whole Cairngorms – maybe all wild land, a Ministry of the Wilderness . . . ?'

Our political leaders may be devoid of a Roosevelt (and for that matter our conservation leaders devoid of a Muir) but as the Scottish-based John Muir Trust pointed out in a 1989 newsletter to members: 'It is significant that when Prince Charles was opening a conference at the Countryside Commission for Scotland headquarters in June he was heard to remark that he was in the John Muir Trust.' Prince Charles is in fact the Trust's patron, and unquestionably the kind of friend in high places which Muir himself would have urged to accompany him on a trek into the wilderness, as he did with Roosevelt in the High Sierras. 'It is only a little trip,' Muir told reporters in San Francisco. 'You can't see much of the Sierras in four days . . . after we get to the valley, the President and I will get lost.'

The problems confronting the Cairngorms today are neatly sum-marised in a sentence which Muir wrote more than a hundred years ago: 'To obtain a hearing on behalf of nature from any standpoint other than that of human use is almost impossible.' But no one clung to that 'almost' with more tenacity than Muir. He protested against the idea that the world 'was made especially for the uses of men. Every animal, plant and crystal controverts it in the plainest terms. Yet it is taught from century to century as something ever new and precious, and in the resulting darkness the enormous conceit is allowed to go unchallenged.' That he challenged it and won his hearing for nature is an achievement for which millions of Americans and the wildest of the American landscape have much to be grateful.

The hour for a new Muir is at hand in the Cairngorms. No one knew more about fighting for the wilderness in the political arena, and no one demonstrated more tellingly how effective such a well-fought fight can be. He won his case because he thought and fought on a scale none had dared to contemplate before him. That lesson awaits a champion in the Cairngorms.

High on Braeriach's plateau, the afternoon slipped into the kind of summer evening which distinguishes itself in the Cairngorms as much for its rarity as its sublimity. The sky drained of almost any colour you could put your finger on, but mustered a show of eggshell shades from off-whitish-blue to off-whitish-yellow. The air warmed as even the breeze fell away. The sounds were of water (the nursery rhymes of the Dee), the sigh of golden plover, and, no matter how intently I concentrated, nothing else at all. I sat for another hour, realised slowly that I had slipped into the brightest antithesis of that darkest mood which imprisoned me in the pinewoods. I had grown through all my Cairngorms years to this moment of closeness to the very rock where I sat. The land lay smiling all around, and I wept at the joy and the privilege of it. However you define your god, it was a sacred hour.

Epilogue

I WALKED DOWN through the evening into Gleann Einich, dawdled along its warm track, where a frog sunned itself, 'hands' across its eyes hide-and-seek style. I stopped by that outpost of the pinewoods that I have invested with the reincarnation of the tree which Seton Gordon identified as Craobh Tillidh, the Tree of the Return, and which stood nearby for centuries. According to Seton Gordon,

> It received its name in the old days when a summer population lived at the head of Gleann Einich, and when the stirks and the cows and their calves were driven up a few days before the people themselves went to the shielings. The herdsman accompanied the animals as far as the Tree of the Return. From here, the beasts, knowing the road from former summers, were able to continue the journey by themselves and the herdsman returned to Rothiemurchus.

Every time I pass the tree heading south I am consigned into the mountain embrace for the duration – an hour, a day, a week. In this embrace, I am in that element in which my step feels surest, in which my instinct feels truest, in which I have something in common with eagles. The mind, like the body, like the eagle – and like the wren – can roam unfettered here, and, like the stirks, go its own way. Judgments and perspectives improve here, and so does the respect for all things wild.

You cannot climb to Loch Coire an Lochain and have the mountain blow you from its old rock reassurances like an autumn leaf and not learn something about the mountain and the leaf.

Every time I pass the tree heading north down into the shadow of the pines, I am the herdsman, my day done, my own return safely gathered in. Like the herdsman, too, I have left my charges behind, for you cannot gather the instincts from the granite of that higher land, shaped by its winds and patrolled by its angles, and herd them tight and obedient into the folds and byres of lesser landscapes. You leave them where they rest most easily, beyond the tree, because from there, 'knowing the road from former summers', they will find their own journeying.

The evening wore a pearly sheen, a pale greying light, a whitening sky. I wanted to share its night and its following dawn, but the morning had been claimed by appointments and arrangements far beyond the Cairngorms. I swithered by the Tree of the Return, then from far up the burn came the voice of a wren. At its beckoning I turned again from the tree and climbed back through the dusk to Lochan Beanaidh, there to share the night and the dawn. That lesser land beyond could wait.

I would be a stirk, a wren, an eagle for a few hours more; I would keep the company of the spirit of the high and lonely places. I sent the herdsman home without me.

Select Bibliography

Brown, Philip, *The Scottish Ospreys*, Heinemann, 1979.

Fox, Stephen, *John Muir and his Legacy*, Little, Brown and Co., 1981.

Gordon, Seton, *The Cairngorm Hills of Scotland*, Cassell, 1925.

Gordon, Seton, *The Golden Eagle*, Collins, 1955, and Melven Press, 1980.

Gray, Affleck, *The Big Grey Man of Ben Macdhui*, Impulse, 1970.

MacCaig, Norman, *Collected Poems*, Chatto and Windus, 1985.

Macrow, Brenda, *Speyside to Deeside*, Oliver and Boyd, 1956.

Nethersole-Thompson, Desmond and Watson, Adam, *The Cairngorms*, Collins, 1974, and Aberdeen University Press, 1981.

Poole, Alan F., *Ospreys – A Natural and Unnatural History*, Cambridge University Press, 1989.

Shepherd, Nan, *The Living Mountain*, Aberdeen University Press, 1977.

Stephen, David, *The World Outside*, Gordon Wright, 1983.

Tomkies, Mike, *A Last Wild Place*, Jonathan Cape, 1984.

Unsworth, Walt, *Everest*, Allen Lane, 1981.

Williams, Heathcote, *Whale Nation*, Jonathan Cape, 1988.

Wood, Wendy, *The Secret of Spey*, Grant and Murray, 1930.